Undeniable

Proof That Only The Christian God Exists

By

William P Thomas

Dedication

This book is dedicated to Ms. Leona M Lanseigne.
Her help was indispensable in the production of this book.

Many thanks, I owe you,
William P Thomas

ISBN-13:978-1726392891
ISBN-10:1726392899

Introduction

As we stumble down the road of life, all of us at one time or another encounter the reality of death. When we see a love one fade away into oblivion, most of us ask the question is this the end or is there hope of a reunion? Is there life after death? It appears, our best hope lies in the scriptures. The Bible says, we can survive death but are the promises of the Bible made by a mortal man or by God?

Acknowledgments

Jay P Green, Sr. and his family, for their generosity and courtesy, in allowing the use of quotes from their interlinear Hebrew Greek English Bible. I can confirm it to be an exact copy of the original Greek New Testament. A letter added to or left out of the original would destroy any acrostic involved.

Leona M Lanseigne, for her assistance with the editing, creating the cover and transmitting this book to the publisher.

Pastor Keith Jones, of the Baptist church in O'Brien, Fl., is a graduate of Trinity Collage of Fl, and Midwestern Baptist Seminary, B.A. in Biblical Studies and a Masters in Theology.

I am indebted to Pastor Jones, for it was he who solved the mystery of the missing letter in the 13th Acrostic!!

What are Acrostics?

Acrostic is a fancy name for a code number.

Acrostics are words hidden in the Scriptures, in this case in the New Testament about 2000 years ago. These writers of the New Testament were ordinary men, fishermen, carpenters, tent-makers, etc. These hidden words, hidden with such precision, couldn't have been done by man. The fact every word, even every letter of the New Testament had to be dictated by Almighty God and only him, him alone! These acrostics are a miracle performed by our Father about 2000 years ago and have remained dormant until now, year 2016! Each acrostic word is hidden by code number. In acrostic
number one the code number is 13.

For example, the Greek word for Jesus is found encoded in Matthew: Chapter 14, Verse 24 in Greek (see Acrostic 1)
It is spelled out in a 13-letter sequence.

We find the first letter of our hidden word, the Greek letter I. Every 13th letter hence will spell Jesus!

Caution!!

When the Greek letter σ is the l last letter of the word it converts to the alternate form ς as seen in Acrostics 4, 6, 8 and 12!

The original New Testament was written in Greek; however, it is not necessary to read or write in Greek in order to verify these acrostics.

Just count the letters!

Acrostic 1

Sequence = number of letters between acrostic letters
Sequence (or code #) in acrostic 1 = 13

Target word is **Jesus**   Greek spelling of Jesus is **Ιησου**

Matthew: Chapter 14, Verse 24 in original Greek

Start Here

μένης, μόνος ἦν ἐκει (24)τὸ δὲ πλοϊον
coming   alone   he was   there. The   and   boat

ἠδη μέσον τῆς θαλάσσης ἦν,βασανιςόμενον
now   amidst   the   sea   was   being   tossed

ὑπὸ των κυμάτων ἦν γὰρ ἐναντίος ὀ
By   the   waves   was   for   contrary   the

Matthew: Chapter 14, Verse 24 in English.

 But the ship was now in the midst of the sea, tossed with waves for
the wind was contrary.

(Large print for seeing impaired) (Interlinear Bible © 1985)

Acrostic 2

Matthew: Chapter 24, Verse 30   Sequence (or code #) = 8

Greek target word is **Jesus**   Greek spelling = **Ιησου**

Start Here

τῶν οὐρανῶν σαλευθήσονται. (30) καί τότε
Of the heavens   be   shaken   and   then

φανήσετάι τό σημεῖον τοῦ υἱοῦ τοῦ
 will appear   the   sign   of   the Son of

ἀνθρωπου ἐν τῶ οὐρανῶ, καί τότε
   man   in   the   heavens   and   then

κόψονται πάσαι αἱ φυλαί τῆς γῆς, καί
will wail   all   the   tribes of the land and

ὀψονται τόν υἱόν του.
They will   see   the Son

Matthew: Chapter 24, Verse 30 in English;

And then will appear the sign of the Son of man in Heaven: And then shall all the tribes of the earth mourn and they shall see the Son.

(Large print for seeing impaired) (Interlinear Bible © 1985)

Acrostic 3

Mark: Chapter 8, Verse 34   Sequence (or code #) = 16

Target word = **Jesus**   Greek spelling = **Ιησου**

Start Here

σταυρὸν αὐτοῦ, καὶ ἀκολουθεί τω μοί. ὁς
  cross of him,   and   let him follow me   who

γάρ ἀν θέλη τὴν ψυχὴν αὐτοῦ σώσαι
for ever desires the   life   of him   to save,

ἀπολέσει αὐτήν ὁς δ ἀν ἀπολέση τήν
shall lose it   who but ever may lose   the

ψυχήν αὐτοῦ ἕνεκεν ἐμοῦ καί τοῦ
life of him   for the sake of me and the

  εὐαγγελίου, οὐτος σώσει
  gospel,   this one will save

Mark: Chapter 8, Verse 35 in English

For whosoever will save his life shall lose it; but whosoever shall lose his life for my sake and the Gospel the same shall save it.

(Large print for seeing impaired) (Interlinear Bible © 1985)

Acrostic 4

Mark: Chapter 13, Verse 32   Sequence (code #) = 17

Target word = **Jesus**   Greek spelling = **Ἰησοῦ**

Start Here

περί δέ τῆς
Concerning but

ἡμέρας ἐκείνης καί τῆς ὥρας οὐδείς οἶδεν,
day   that   and the   hour no one   knows,

οὐδέ οἱ ἄγγελοι οἱ ἐν οὐρανώ, οὐδέ ὁ υἱός,
not   the angels those in Heaven, nor the Son,

εἰ μή ὁ πατήρ. (33) βλέπετε, ἀγρυπνεῖτε
except the Father.   Look out!   Be wakeful.

Mark: Chapter 13, Verse 32 in English

But of that day and that hour knoweth no man, no, not the angels which
are in Heaven, neither the Son but the Father

(Large print for seeing impaired) (Interlinear Bible © 1985)

Acrostic 5

Luke: Chapter 9, Verse 23 and 24
Sequence (or code #) = 16

Target word = **Jesus**   Greek spelling = **Ιησου**

Start Here

καί άκολουθείτω μοι.(24) ός γάρ άν
And let him follow   Me whoever   for   may

θέλη τήν ψυχήν αύτοΰ σώσαι, άπολέσει
Desire the   life   of him to save, he will lose it

αύτήν. ος δ άν άπολέση τήν ψυχήν αύτοΰ
Whoever but may lose   the   life   of him

ενεκεν έμοΰ, ούτος σώσει
For the sake of me this one will save

Luke Verse 24 in English;

For whosoever will save his life shall lose it: but whosoever will lose his life for my sake, the same shall save it.

(Large print for seeing impaired) (Interlinear Bible © 1985)

Acrostic 6

John: Chapter 4, Verse 5 and 6   Sequence (or code #) =18

Target word = **Jesus**   Greek spelling = **Ἰήσου**

(5) ἔρχεται ουν εἰς πόλιν τῆς Σαμαρείας λεγομένην
He comes   then   unto   a city of   Samaria   being called

Συχαρ, πλήσίον τοῦ χωρίου ὁ ἐδωκεν Ιακώβ
Sychar   near   the piece of land   that had given   Jacob

Start Here

Ιωσῆφ τῶ υιῶ αὐτοῦ (6) ἤν δὲ ἐκεῖ πηγή τοῦ
to Joseph the son   of him   was and there a fountain

Ιακώβ. ὁ οὖν Ιησοῦς κεκοπιακὼς ἐκ τῆς ὁδοιπορίας
of Jacob.   Then   Jesus   being wearied from   the   journey

ἐκαθέςετο ουτως ἐπί τῆ πηγή ὠρα ἤν ωσει
was sitting   thus   on   the well the hour was about

John: Chapter 4, Verse 5 in English.

Then cometh He to a city of Sychar near to the parcel, that Jacob gave
to his son Joseph.
(6) Now Jacob's well was there, Jesus therefore, being wearied with His
journey, sat thus on the well: and it was about the 6th hour.

Acrostic # 7

John: Chapter 21, Verse 17   Sequence (or code #) = 7

Target word = **Jesus**   Greek spelling = **Ιησου**

Start Here

φιλώ σε. λέγει αὐτώ ὁ Iησοῦς, βόσκε τά
I love you   says   to him Jesus   feed   the

προβατά μου
sheep   of me

John: Chapter 21, Verse 17 in English.

I love thee, Jesus saith unto him, feed my sheep.

(Large print for seeing impaired) (Interlinear Bible © 1985)

Acrostic 8

Romans: Chapter 8, Verse 34 and 35
Sequence (or code #) = 22

Target word = **Jesus**   Greek spelling = **Ιησου**

Start Here

Θεου, ὁς και ἐντυγχάνει ὑπὲρ ἡμῶν. (35) τίς
of God who also intercedes on behalf of us.   Who

ἡμάς χωρίσει ἀπὸ τῆς ἀγάπης τοῦ Χριστοῦ;
 us will separate from   the   love   of   Christ

θλῖψις, ἡ στενοχωρία , ἡ διωγμός, ἡ

shall trouble, or distress,   or persecution, or

λιμός, ἡ γυμνότης, ἡ κίνδυνος, ἡ μάχαιρα;
famine or nakedness, or   danger,   or sword

(36) καθως γέγραπται
Even as it has   been written

End of verse 34 and all of verse 35 in English,

of God, who also maketh. Intercession for us.
Verse 35; Who shall separate us from the love of Christ? Shall tribuiation, or famine, or nakedness, or peril, of sword?

(Large print for seeing impaired) (Interlinear Bible © 1985)

Acrostic 9

Colossians: Chapter 3, Verse 11
Sequence (or code # =10)

Target word = **Jesus**   Greek spelling = **Ιησου**

Start Here

(11) ὁπου οὐκ ἐνι Ἐλλην καί Ιουδαιός, περιτομη
    Where not there is Greek and Jew circumcision

και ἀκροβυστία, βάρβαρος, Σκύθης, δουλος,
and uncircumcision, foreigner, Scythian, slave,

ἐλεύθερος ἀλλά τά πάντα καί ἐν πάσι Χριστός
(or) freeman, but all things and in all Christ is.

Colossians: Chapter 3, Verse 11 in English.

Where there is neither Greek nor Jew, circumcision nor
uncircumcision, Barbarian, Scyth'i-an, bond nor free but
Christ is all in all.

(Large print for seeing impaired) (Interlinear Bible © 1985)

Acrostic 10

Galatians: Chapter 3, Verse 27
Sequence (or code #) = 17

Target word = **Jesus**   Greek spelling = **Ιησου**

Start Here

(27) ὅσοι γὰρ εἰς Χριστόν ἐβαπτί σθηιε, Χριστόν
As   many   as for   into Christ were baptized   Christ

ἐνεδύσασθε (28) οὐκ ἐνι Ἰουδαῖος οὐδὲ Ἕλλήν,
you put on not   there is   Jew   nor   Greek

οὐκ ἐνι δουλος οὐδὲ ἐλευθερος, οὐκ ἐνι ἀρσεν
 not there is slave   nor freeman,   not there is   male

καὶ θήλυ πάντες
 and   female,   all

Galatians: Chapter 3 Verse 27 in English.

For as many of you as have been baptized into Christ have put on
Christ. (28) There is neither Jew nor Greek, there is neither bond nor
free, there is neither male nor female.

(Large print for seeing impaired) (Interlinear Bible © 1985)

Acrostic 11

First John: Chapter 3, Verse 17   Sequence (or code #) = 13

Target word = **Jesus**   Greek spelling = **Ιησου**

Start Here

τιθέναι, (17)ὁς δ ἀν ἐχη τον βίον τοῦ κόσμου,
lay down   whoever has   the means of life of   the world

και θεωρή τον ἀδελφὸν αὐτου χρείαν ἐχοντα,
and beholds   the brother   of him   need   having,

καί κλείση τα σπλάγχνα
and   shuts up   the   bowels

First John: Chapter 3, Verse 17 in English.

But whoso hath this worlds good, and seeth his brother have need and shutteth up his bowels

(Large print for seeing impaired) (Interlinear Bible © 1985)

Acrostic 12

Jude: Chapter 1, Verse 4

Target word = **Jesus**

Sequence (or code #) = 20

Greek spelling = **Ιησου**

Jude: Chapter 1, Verse 4 in Greek

Start Here

γραμμένοί εἰς τουτο το κρίμα, ἀσεβείς, τὴν
Been written before   to this   judgement , ungodly (ones) the

τοῦ Θεοῦ ημὼν χάριν μετατιθέντες εἰς
of the God   of us grace   perverting   into

ἀσέλγειαν, καὶ τον μονον δεσπότην Θεόν,
unbridled lust,   and the   only   master God

καὶ Κυριον ἡμών Ιησοϋν Χριστόν ἀρνούμενοι
and   Lord   of us   Jesus   Christ   denying

Jude: Chapter 1, Verse 4 in English

For there are certain men crept in unawares who were before of old ordained to this condemnation, ungodly men, turning the grace of our God into lasciviousness, and denying the only Lord God, and our Lord Jesus Christ.

(Large print for seeing impaired) (Interlinear Bible © 1985)

Acrostic 13

Matthew 27 verse 9, 10 &11   Sequence (or code) = 41
Target word = **Jesus**   Greek spelling = Ιησου

(9) Τότε ἐπληρώθη τό ρηθέν διά Ἱερεμίου του, προφήτου, λέΥοντος
Then was   fulfilled that   spoken through Jeremiah   the
 prophet   saying

Start Here

Καί ἔλαβον τά τριάκοντα ἀργύρια, τήν τιμήν τού τετιμημένου,
and I took   the   thirty   pieces of silver the price of the one
having been priced

ὁν ἐτιμήσαντο ἀπό υἱων Ἱσραήλ (10) καί ἐδωκαν αὐτά εἰς
whom they priced from sons   of Israel   and   gave   them
for

τόν ἀγρόν τοΰ κεραμέως, καθά συνέταζέ(ν)[1] μοι Κύριος
the   field of the potter as   directed   me   the Lord

(11) Ο δέ Ἱησοΰς ἐστη ἐμπροσθεν τοΰ ἡγεμόνος· καί ἐπηρώτησεν
        and Jesus   stood   before   the   governor   and
questioned

αὐτόν ὁ ἡγεμών, λέγων, συ εἴ ὁ βασιλεύς τῶν Ἱουδαίων
him   the governor saying, you are the king of the   Jews

1 = For appendix 1, see next page.

Appendix 1

In Mr. William Thomas' book on Bible Acrostics, he asked me why the last one, the 13th, did not add up as did all the others. I began to research and found that some Greek Texts add a letter in Matthew 27:10 and other Greek Texts do not add a letter. The word in particular is the word "suntaxen – συνεταξεν" which is the transliteration of "suntasso – συντάσσω" and is translated directed or appointed. I found two Greek Texts do not have the last letter, the letter "nu" in their text. The Nestle-Aland, the Textus Receptus as translated by Elzevir, Griesbach, Lachmann, Tischendorf, Tregelles, Alford, and Wordsworth, add the letter "nu." Since Mr. Thomas is using the interlinear by Jay Green, Sr., the text does not add the letter "nu." This makes his acrostic fail because of the lack of this one letter. However, the more modern texts do add the letter and this makes his acrostics succeed. In my humble opinion as long as the reader is told about this difference, Mr. Thomas is within his rights to use another Greek Text to make the acrostic fit. The difference does not take away from his original intent in any way.

Sincerely,
Pastor Keith Jones

All of the Greek New Testament quotes used here are from "The Interlinear Greek-English New Testament Volume 4" by Jay P Green, Sr.

Available at S. G. P. Books.com, 307 S Glick St., PO Box 491, Mulberry, In 46058 or at Amazon.com.

Heaven and earth shall pass away but my words shall not pass away. St. Matthew: Chapter 24, Verse 35.

Greek Alphabet
From Wikipedia, the free encyclopedia.

Αα	Alpha			Νν	Nu	
Ββ	Beta			Ξξ	Xi	
Γγ	Gamma			Οο	Omicron 4	ο
Δδ	Delta			Ππ	Pi	
Εε	Epsilon			Ρρ	Rho	
Ζζ	Zeta			Σσς	Sigma 3	σ
Ηη	Eta 2	η		Ττ	Tau	
Θθ	Theta			Υυ	Upsilon 5	υ
Ιι	Iota 1	Ι		Φφ	Phi	
Κκ	Kappa			Χχ	Chi	
Λλ	Lambda			Ψψ	Psi	
Μμ	Mu			Ωω	Omega	

Caution!! (σ) and (ς) are two different forms of the letter Sigma.
When (σ) is the last letter of a word, it converts to the alternate form (ς) as will be seen in acrostics 4, 6, 8 and 12.

Large print for seeing impaired

	Chapter	Verse	Sequence
Matthew	14	24	13
Matthew	24	30	8
Mark	8	34	16
Mark	13	32	17
Luke	9	23	16
John	4	5	18
John	21	17	7
Romans	8	34	22
Galations	3	27	17
Colossians	3	11	10
First John	3	17	13
Jude	1	4	20

Book of the Bible
Chapter
Verse
Sequence = Number of letters between acrostics.

Large print for seeing impaired

Conclusion

These are 13 acrostics spelling the name (Ιησου). There may be More but these are enough to prove the Bible is the word of God. I believe we will find many more acrostics by using other target words. I feel we have only scratched the surface.

The odds of one of these acrostics happening by chance is about 3000 to one, by my calculation. The odds that all 13 acrostics are by chance is about one in 36000.

When we consider the fact that these acrostics were placed in the scriptures about 2000 years ago by fishermen, carpenters, tax-collectors, tent-makers, etc. there is no way any of these writers could have accomplished this without the help of Almighty God!

All writers of the New Testament, except Peter and James are endorsed by God! I say, based on the fact, that they have acrostics naming Jesus in code, within their books, it is the signature of The Lord!

Peter was endorsed by God in acrostic 7, saying to Peter, "feed my sheep." This leaves only James, who I believe will be endorsed by later acrostics.

So, for all you atheists and agnostics here is your proof. You can accept it or you can go to hell!

May God have mercy,
    With respect
    W. P. Thomas

Acrostic Index

The following is the full Chapter, in Greek and in English. In Matthew: Chapter 14, Verse 24, where acrostic 1 begins, is clearly marked.

1 At that time Herod the tetrarch heard the fame of Jesus.
2 And he said to his servants, This is John the Baptist. He is risen from the dead, and because of this, powerful works (are) working in him.

3. For seizing John, Herod bound him and put (him) into prison, because of Herodias, the wife of his brother Philip.

4 For John said to him, It is not lawful for you to have her.
5 And desiring to kill him, he feared the crowd, because they held him as a prophet.
6 But a birthday (feast for) Herod being held, the daughter of Herodias danced in the midst

```
      1722   1565   3588  2540           191          2264    3588   5076            3588
1. Ἐν   ἐκείνῳ  τῷ  καιρῷ  ἤκουσεν Ἡρώδης  ὁ  τετραάρχης  τὴν
      At     that          time     heard    Herod      the tetrarch    the

189        2424           2532 2036 3588   3816      846          3778       2076
ἀκοὴν  Ἰησοῦ, 2 καὶ  εἶπε  τοῖς  παισὶν  αὐτοῦ,  Οὗτός  ἐστιν
fame    of Jesus,      and said  to the   servants  of him,     This        is

2491        3588    910         846        1453      575 3588    3498       2532
Ἰωάννης  ὁ  βαπτιστής·  αὐτὸς  ἠγέρθη  ἀπὸ τῶν νεκρῶν,  καὶ
John         the Baptist;         he is    risen    from the   dead,       and

1223 5124 3588  1411           1754          1722 846      3588 1063  2264
διὰ τοῦτο αἱ δυνάμεις ἐνεργοῦσιν ἐν αὐτῷ. 3 ὁ γὰρ Ἡρώδης
because of this the works of power operate  in  him.          For    Herod

2902          3588   291         1210       846 2532  5087    1722 5438
κρατήσας  τὸν Ἰωάννην  ἔδησεν αὐτὸν καὶ  ἔθετο  ἐν φυλακῇ,
having seized    John        bound    him  and    put in    prison,

1223       2266      3588   1135        5376         3588   80          846
διὰ Ἡρωδιάδα  τὴν γυναῖκα Φιλίππου τοῦ ἀδελφοῦ αὐτοῦ.
because of Herodias the      wife      of Philip    the   brother    of him.

3004     1063 846 3588 2491        3756     1832   4671   2192      846
4 ἔλεγε γὰρ αὐτῷ ὁ Ἰωάννης, Οὐκ ἔξεστί σοι ἔχειν αὐτήν.
  said    For to him  John,         Not  it is lawful for you to have  her.

2532  2309    846       615              5399      3588  3793   3754 5613
5 καὶ θέλων  αὐτὸν ἀποκτεῖναι, ἐφοβήθη τὸν ὄχλον, ὅτι ὡς
  And wishing  him     to kill,          he feared  the   crowd, because as

4396        846    2192      1077     1161  71      3588 · 2264
προφήτην αὐτὸν εἶχον. 6 γενεσίων δὲ ἀγομένων τοῦ Ἡρώδου,
a prophet   him they held. a birth-feast But being held     of Herod,

3738         3588  2364   3588     2266        1722 3588 3319   2532
ὠρχήσατο  ἡ  θυγάτηρ τῆς Ἡρωδιάδος ἐν τῷ μέσῳ,  καὶ
danced        the  daughter       of Herodias  in  the midst,  and
```

1 At that time Herod the tetrarch heard of the fame of Jesus,
2 And said unto his servants, This is John the Baptist; he is risen from the dead; and therefore mighty works do shew forth themselves in him.

3. For Herod had laid hold on John, and bound him, and put (him) in prison for Herodias' sake, his brother Philip's wife.

4 For John said unto him, It is not lawful for thee to have her,
5 And when he would have put him to death, he feared the multitude, because they counted him as a prophet.
6 But when Herod's birthday was kept, the daughter of Herodias danced before them,

---

Center interlinear (Strong's numbers / Greek / English):

700 3588 2264   3526 3326 3727   3670   846 1325
ἤρεσε τῷ Ἡρῴδῃ. 7 ὅθεν μεθ᾽ ὅρκου ὡμολόγησεν αὐτῇ δοῦναι
pleased Herod. From which with an oath he assented to her to give

3588 1437 154   3588 1161   4264   5259 3588 3384
ὃ ἐὰν αἰτήσηται. 8 ἡ δὲ, προβιβασθεῖσα ὑπὸ τῆς μητρὸς
whatever she might ask. she But, being urged on by the mother

846 1325 3427 5346 5602 1909 4094 3588 2776   2491
αὐτῆς, Δός μοι, φησίν, ὧδε ἐπὶ πίνακι τὴν κεφαλὴν Ἰωάννου
of her, Give me, she says, here on a platter the head of John

3588 910   2532 3076 3588 935   1223 1161 3588 3727
τοῦ βαπτιστοῦ. 9 καὶ ἐλυπήθη ὁ βασιλεύς, διὰ δὲ τοὺς ὅρκους
the Baptist. And was grieved the king, because but of the oaths

2532 3588   4873   2753   1325   2532 3992
καὶ τοὺς συνανακειμένους, ἐκέλευσε δοθῆναι· 10 καὶ πέμψας
and those reclining with (him) he ordered (it) to be given And sending

607   3588 2491   1722 3588 5438   2532 5342 3588
ἀπεκεφάλισε τὸν Ἰωάννην ἐν τῇ φυλακῇ· 11 καὶ ἠνέχθη ἡ
He beheaded John in the prison. And was brought the

2776 846 1909 4094 2532 1325 3588 2877   2532 5342
κεφαλὴ αὐτοῦ ἐπὶ πίνακι, καὶ ἐδόθη τῷ κορασίῳ· καὶ ἤνεγκε
head of him on a platter, and was given to the girl, and she brought

3588 3384 846   2532   4334   3588 3101   846 142
τῇ μητρὶ αὐτῆς. 12 καὶ προσελθόντες οἱ μαθηταὶ αὐτοῦ ἦραν
to the mother of her. And having come near the disciples of him took

3588 4983 2532 2290 846 2532 2064   518   3588
τὸ σῶμα, καὶ ἔθαψαν αὐτό· καὶ ἐλθόντες ἀπήγγειλαν τῷ
the body, and buried it, and coming told

2424
Ἰησοῦ.
Jesus

2532 191 3588 2424   402   1564 1722 4143 1519
13. Καὶ ἀκούσας ὁ Ἰησοῦς ἀνεχώρησεν ἐκεῖθεν ἐν πλοίῳ εἰς
And hearing Jesus withdrew from there in a boat into

2948 5117 2596 2398 2532 191   3588 3793   190
ἔρημον τόπον κατ᾽ ἰδίαν· καὶ ἀκούσαντες οἱ ὄχλοι ἠκολού-
a deserted place privately And having heard the crowds followed

846 3979 575 3588 4172   2532   1831   3588 2424
θησαν αὐτῷ πεζῇ ἀπὸ τῶν πόλεων. 14 καὶ ἐξελθὼν ὁ Ἰησοῦς
Him on foot from the cities. And going out Jesus

1492 4183 3793 2532 4697   1909 846 2532
εἶδε πολὺν ὄχλον, καὶ ἐσπλαγχνίσθη ἐπ᾽ αὐτούς, καὶ ἐθερά-
saw a great crowd, and was filled with pity on them, and He

2323 3588 732   846   3798 1161 1096
πευσε τοὺς ἀρρώστους αὐτῶν. 15 ὀψίας δὲ γενομένης,
healed the infirm of them. evening And having come,

4334 846 3588 3101 846   3004   2048
προσῆλθον αὐτῷ οἱ μαθηταὶ αὐτοῦ, λέγοντες, Ἔρημός
came near to Him the disciples of Him, saying, Deserted

2076 3588 5117   2532 3588 5610 2235   3928   630   3588
ἐστιν ὁ τόπος, καὶ ἡ ὥρα ἤδη παρῆλθεν· ἀπόλυσον τοὺς
is the place, and the hour already is gone by. Dismiss the

3793 2443 565   1519 3588 2968   59   1438
ὄχλους, ἵνα ἀπελθόντες εἰς τὰς κώμας ἀγοράσωσιν ἑαυτοῖς
crowds, that going away into the villages they may buy for themselves

1033   3588 1161 2424   2036 846 3756 5532   2192
βρώματα. 16 ὁ δὲ Ἰησοῦς εἶπεν αὐτοῖς, Οὐ χρείαν ἔχουσιν
foods. But Jesus said to them, Not need they have

565   1325 846 5210 5315   3588 1161 3004   846
ἀπελθεῖν· δότε αὐτοῖς ὑμεῖς φαγεῖν. 17 οἱ δὲ λέγουσιν αὐτῷ,
to go away, give to them you to eat. they But say to Him,

3756 2192 5602 1487 3361 4002 740   2532 1417 2486   3588 1161 2036
Οὐκ ἔχομεν ὧδε εἰ μὴ πέντε ἄρτους καὶ δύο ἰχθύας. 18 ὁ δὲ εἶπε,
Not we have here except five loaves and two fish. He And said,

---

Literal Translation (left column):

and pleased Herod.
7 From which (act) he assented with an oath to give her whatever she should ask.
8 But she being urged on by her mother, she says, Give me here on a platter the head of John the Baptist.
9 And the king was grieved, but because of the oaths, and those reclining with (him), he ordered (it) to be given.
10 And sending, he beheaded John in the prison.
11 And his head was brought on a platter and was given to the girl, and she brought (it) to her mother.
12 And having come, his disciples took the body and buried it; and coming, (they) reported to Jesus.

13. And having heard, Jesus withdrew privately from there in a boat, into a deserted place. And hearing, the crowds followed Him on foot out of the cities.
14 And going out, Jesus saw a great crowd and was filled with pity on them. And He healed their infirm ones.

15. And evening coming, His disciples came near to Him, saying, The place is deserted, and the hour is already gone by. Dismiss the crowds, that going away into the villages they may buy provisions for themselves.

16 But Jesus said to them, They have no need to go away. You give them (food) to eat.
17 But they said to Him, We have nothing here except five loaves and two fish.
18 And He said,

King James Version (right column):

and pleased Herod.
7 Whereupon he promised with an oath to give her whatsoever she would ask.
8 And she, being before instructed of her mother, said, Give me here John Baptist's head in a charger.
9 And the king was sorry: nevertheless for the oath's sake, and them which sat with him at meat, he commanded (it) to be given (her).
10 And he sent, and beheaded John in the prison.
11 And his head was brought in a charger, and given to the damsel: and she brought (it) to her mother.
12 And his disciples came, and took up the body, and buried it, and went and told Jesus.

13. When Jesus heard (of it), he departed thence by ship into a desert place apart: and when the people had heard (thereof), they followed him on foot out of the cities.
14 And Jesus went forth, and saw a great multitude, and was moved with compassion toward them, and he healed their sick.
15. And when it was evening, his disciples came to him, saying, This is a desert place, and the time is now past; send the multitude away, that they may go into the villages, and buy themselves victuals.

16 But Jesus said unto them, They need not depart; give ye them to eat.
17 And they say unto him, We have here but five loaves, and two fishes.
18 He said,

Literal Translation

Bring them here to Me.
19 And commanding the crowds to recline on the grass, and taking the five loaves and two fish, looking up to Heaven, He blessed. And breaking, He gave the loaves to the disciples, and the disciples (gave) to the crowds.

20 And all ate and were satisfied. And they took up the left over pieces, twelve hand-baskets full.

21 And the ones eating were about five thousand men, besides women and children.

22. And immediately Jesus made His disciples get into a boat and to go before Him to the other side until He should dismiss the crowds.

23 And having dismissed the crowds, He went up into the mountain alone to pray. And evening coming on, He was there alone.

24 But the boat was now in (the) middle of the sea, tossed by the waves, for the wind was contrary.

25 But in the fourth watch of the night, Jesus went out to them, walking on the sea.

26 And seeing Him walking on the sea, the disciples were troubled, saying, It is a phantom! And they cried out from the fear.

27 But immediately Jesus spoke to them, saying, Be comforted! I AM! Do not fear.

28 And answering Him, Peter said, Lord, if You are, command me to come to You on the waters.

29 And He said,

Interlinear (Greek text with Strong's numbers)

5342 3427 846 5602 2532 2753 3588 3793 347
φέρετέ μοι αὐτούς ὧδε. 19 καὶ κελεύσας τοὺς ὄχλους ἀνακλι-
Bring to Me them here. And commanding the crowds to recline

1909 3588 5528 2532 2983 3588 4002 740 2532 3588
θῆναι ἐπὶ τοὺς χόρτους, καὶ λαβὼν τοὺς πέντε ἄρτους καὶ τοὺς
on the grass, and taking the five loaves and the

1417 2486 308 1519 3588 3772 2127 2532
δύο ἰχθύας, ἀναβλέψας εἰς τὸν οὐρανόν, εὐλόγησε, καὶ
two fish, looking up into Heaven, He blessed, and

2806 1325 3588 3101 3588 740 3588 1161 3101 3588
κλάσας ἔδωκε τοῖς μαθηταῖς τοὺς ἄρτους, οἱ δὲ μαθηταὶ τοῖς
breaking He gave to the disciples the loaves, the and disciples to the

3793 2532 5315 3956 2532 5526 2532 142 3588
ὄχλοις. 20 καὶ ἔφαγον πάντες, καὶ ἐχορτάσθησαν· καὶ ἦραν τὸ
crowds. And ate all, and were satisfied, and they took the

4052 3588 2801 1427 2894 4134 3588
περισσεῦον τῶν κλασμάτων, δώδεκα κοφίνους πλήρεις. 21 οἱ
left over of the pieces, twelve hand-baskets full. those

1161 2068 2258 435 5616 4000 5565 1135
δὲ ἐσθίοντες ἦσαν ἄνδρες ὡσεὶ πεντακισχίλιοι, χωρὶς γυναι-
And eating were men about five thousand, apart from women

2532 3813
κῶν καὶ παιδίων.
and children.

2532 2112 315 3588 2424 3588 3101 846
22. Καὶ εὐθέως ἠνάγκασεν ὁ Ἰησοῦς τοὺς μαθητὰς αὐτοῦ
And instantly constrained Jesus the disciples of Him

1684 1519 3588 4143 2532 4254 846 1519 3588 4008
ἐμβῆναι εἰς τὸ πλοῖον, καὶ προάγειν αὐτὸν εἰς τὸ πέραν,
to enter into the boat, and to go before Him to the other side,

2193 3759 630 3588 3793 2532 630 3588 3793
ἕως οὗ ἀπολύσῃ τοὺς ὄχλους. 23 καὶ ἀπολύσας τοὺς ὄχλους,
until He dismissed the crowds. And having dismissed the crowds

305 1519 3588 3735 2596 2398 4336 3798 1161 1096
ἀνέβη εἰς τὸ ὄρος κατ' ἰδίαν προσεύξασθαι. ὀψίας δὲ γενο-
He went into the mountain apart in order to pray. evening And

3441 2258 1563 3588 1161 4143 2235 3319 3588 2281
μένης, μόνος ἦν ἐκεῖ. 24 τὸ δὲ πλοῖον ἤδη μέσον τῆς θαλάσσης
coming. alone He was there. the And boat now amidst the sea

2258 928 5259 3588 2949 2258 1063 1727 3588
ἦν, βασανιζόμενον ὑπὸ τῶν κυμάτων· ἦν γὰρ ἐναντίος ὁ
was, being tossed by the waves; was for contrary the

417 5067 1161 5438 3588 3571 565 4314 846
ἄνεμος. 25 τετάρτη δὲ φυλακῇ τῆς νυκτὸς ἀπῆλθε πρὸς αὐτοὺς
wind in (the) fourth But watch of the night went toward them

3588 2424 4043 1909 3588 2281 2532 1492 846
ὁ Ἰησοῦς, περιπατῶν ἐπὶ τῆς θαλάσσης. 26 καὶ ἰδόντες αὐτὸν
Jesus, walking on the sea. And seeing Him

3588 3101 1909 3588 2281 4043 5015
οἱ μαθηταὶ ἐπὶ τὴν θάλασσαν περιπατοῦντα ἐταράχθησαν,
the disciples on the sea walking about they were troubled,

3004 3754 5326 2076 2532 575 3588 5401 2896
λέγοντες ὅτι Φάντασμά ἐστι· καὶ ἀπὸ τοῦ φόβου ἔκραξαν.
saying, A phantom it is, and out of fear they cried out.

2112 1161 2980 846 3588 2424 3004 2291 1473
27 εὐθέως δὲ ἐλάλησεν αὐτοῖς ὁ Ἰησοῦς, λέγων, Θαρσεῖτε, ἐγώ
at once But spoke to them Jesus, saying, Be comforted, I

1510 3361 5399 611 1161 846 3588 4074 2036 2962
εἰμι· μὴ φοβεῖσθε. 28 ἀποκριθεὶς δὲ αὐτῷ ὁ Πέτρος εἶπε, Κύριε,
AM! not Do fear. answering And Him, Peter said, Lord,

1487 4771 1488 2753 3165 4314 4571 2064 1909 3588 5204 3588 1161 2036
εἰ σὺ εἶ, κέλευσόν με πρός σε ἐλθεῖν ἐπὶ τὰ ὕδατα· 29 ὁ δὲ εἶπεν,
If You are, command me to You to come on the waters He And said,

---

King James Version

Bring them hither to me.
19 And he commanded the multitude to sit down on the grass, and took the five loaves, and the two fishes, and looking up to heaven, he blessed, and brake, and gave the loaves to (his) disciples, and the disciples to the multitude.

20 And they did all eat, and were filled: and they took up of the fragments that remained twelve baskets full.

21 And they that had eaten were about five thousand men, beside women and children.

22. And straightway Jesus constrained his disciples to get into a ship, and to go before him unto the other side, while he sent the multitudes away.

23 And when he had sent the multitudes away, he went up into a mountain apart to pray: and when the evening was come, he was there alone.

24 But the ship was now in the midst of the sea, tossed with waves: for the wind was contrary.

25 And in the fourth watch of the night Jesus went unto them, walking on the sea.

26 And when the disciples saw him walking on the sea, they were troubled, saying, It is a spirit; and they cried out for fear.

27 But straightway Jesus spake unto them, saying, Be of good cheer; it is I; be not afraid.

28 And Peter answered him and said, Lord, if it be thou, bid me come unto thee on the water.

29 And he said,

| Literal Translation | Matthew 14:30 | King James Version |

Literal Translation

Come! And going down from the boat, Peter walked on the waters to come to Jesus. 30 But seeing the wind strong, he was afraid, and beginning to sink, he cried out, saying, Lord, save me!

31 And immediately stretching out the hand, Jesus took hold of him, and says to him, Little-faith, why did you doubt?

32 And they going up into the boat, the wind ceased.

33 And those in the boat came and worshiped Him, saying, Truly, You are the Son of God.

34. And having passed over, they came to the land of Gennesaret. 35 And recognizing Him, the men of that place sent to all that neighborhood, and brought to Him all those badly ill. 36 And (they) begged Him that they might only touch the fringe of His garment. And as many as touched were cured.

Greek Interlinear

2064 2532 2597 575 3588 4143 3588 4074 4043
Ἐλθέ. καὶ καταβὰς ἀπὸ τοῦ πλοίου ὁ Πέτρος περιεπάτησεν
Come! And descending from the boat Peter walked

1909 3588 5204 2064 4314 3588 2424 991 1161 3588
ἐπὶ τὰ ὕδατα, ἐλθεῖν πρὸς τὸν Ἰησοῦν. 30 βλέπων δὲ τὸν
on the waters, to come to Jesus. seeing But the

417 2478 5399 2532 756 2670
ἄνεμον ἰσχυρὸν ἐφοβήθη· καὶ ἀρξάμενος καταποντίζεσθαι
wind strong, he was afraid, and beginning to sink

2896 3004 2962 4982 3165 2112 1161 3588 2424 1614
ἔκραξε, λέγων, Κύριε, σῶσόν με. 31 εὐθέως δὲ ὁ Ἰησοῦς ἐκτείνας
he cried out, saying, Lord, save me. instantly And Jesus stretching out

3588 5495 1949 846 2532 3004 846 3640
τὴν χεῖρα ἐπελάβετο αὐτοῦ καὶ λέγει αὐτῷ, Ὀλιγόπιστε,
the hand took hold of him, and says to him, Little-faith,

1519 5101 1365 2532 1684 846 1519 3588 4143
εἰς τί ἐδίστασας; 32 καὶ ἐμβάντων αὐτῶν εἰς τὸ πλοῖον,
why did you doubt? And going up they into the boat,

2869 3588 417 3588 1161 1722 3588 4143 2064
ἐκόπασεν ὁ ἄνεμος. 33 οἱ δὲ ἐν τῷ πλοίῳ ἐλθόντες
ceased the wind. the (ones) And in the boat coming

4352 846 3004 230 2316 5207 1488
προσεκύνησαν αὐτῷ, λέγοντες, Ἀληθῶς Θεοῦ υἱός εἶ.
worshiped Him, saying, Truly of God Son You are.

2532 1276 2064 1519 3588 1093 1082 2532
34. Καὶ διαπεράσαντες ἦλθον εἰς τὴν γῆν Γεννησαρέτ. 35 καὶ
And passing over they came into the land of Gennesaret And

1921 846 3588 435 3588 5117 1565 649
ἐπιγνόντες αὐτὸν οἱ ἄνδρες τοῦ τόπου ἐκείνου ἀπέστειλαν
recognizing Him the men of place that sent

1519 3650 3588 4066 1565 2532 4374 846
εἰς ὅλην τὴν περίχωρον ἐκείνην, καὶ προσήνεγκαν αὐτῷ
into all the neighborhood that, and brought to Him

3956 3588 2560 2192 2532 3870 846 2443
πάντας τοὺς κακῶς ἔχοντας, 36 καὶ παρεκάλουν αὐτὸν, ἵνα
all those badly ill having, and begged Him that

3440 680 3588 2899 3588 2440 846 2532
μόνον ἅψωνται τοῦ κρασπέδου τοῦ ἱματίου αὐτοῦ· καὶ
only they might touch the fringe of the garment of Him, and

3745 680 1295
ὅσοι ἥψαντο διεσώθησαν.
as many as touched were cured

King James Version

Come. And when Peter was come down out of the ship, he walked on the water, to go to Jesus. 30 But when he saw the wind boisterous, he was afraid; and beginning to sink, he cried, saying, Lord, save me.

31 And immediately Jesus stretched forth (his) hand, and caught him, and said unto him, O thou of little faith, wherefore didst thou doubt?

32 And when they were come into the ship, the wind ceased.

33 Then they that were in the ship came and worshipped him, saying, Of a truth thou art the Son of God.

34. And when they were gone over, they came into the land of Gennesaret. 35 And when the men of that place had knowledge of him, they sent out into all that country round about, and brought unto him all that were diseased; 36 And besought him that they might only touch the hem of his garment: and as many as touched were made perfectly whole.

Acrostic Index

The following is the full chapter in English and in Greek of Matthew: Chapter 24, Verse 30, where acrostic 2 begins, is clearly marked.

Matthew 24

1. And going out, Jesus went away from the temple. And His disciples came to show Him the buildings of the temple.

```
2532   1831    3588   2424        4198          575 3588  2411   2532
1. Καὶ ἐξελθὼν ὁ Ἰησοῦς ἐπορεύετο ἀπὸ τοῦ ἱεροῦ· καὶ
   And  going forth  Jesus   went away   from the  temple  and
4334        3588 3101      846    1925      846 3588      3619
προσῆλθον οἱ μαθηταὶ αὐτοῦ ἐπιδεῖξαι αὐτῷ τὰς οἰκοδομὰς
came up    the disciples of Him  to show  Him the   buildings
3588   2411     3588 1161 2424   2036     846      3756  991    3956
τοῦ ἱεροῦ. 2 ὁ δὲ Ἰησοῦς εἶπεν αὐτοῖς, Οὐ βλέπετε πάντα
of the Temple.  And  Jesus    said   to them, Not  you see  all
5023    281    3004  5213   3756 3361 863     5602 3037  1909 3037 3739
ταῦτα; ἀμὴν λέγω ὑμῖν, οὐ μὴ ἀφεθῇ ὧδε λίθος ἐπὶ λίθον, ὃς
these?  Truly  I say  to you, Not at all will be left here stone on stone which
3756 3361  2647
οὐ μὴ καταλυθήσεται.
not at all shall be thrown down.
```

2 But Jesus said to them, Do you not see all these things? Truly I say to you, There will not at all be left one stone on a stone which in no way will not be thrown down.

```
2521       1161 846  1909 3588 3735   3588  1636    4334
3. Καθημένου δὲ αὐτοῦ ἐπὶ τοῦ ὄρους τῶν ἐλαιῶν, προσῆλ-
   sitting   And  He   on  the  Mount of the Olives,  came
846 3588 3101   2596  2398     3004         2036   2254  4129
θον αὐτῷ οἱ μαθηταὶ κατ᾽ ἰδίαν, λέγοντες, Εἰπὲ ἡμῖν, πότε
up  to Him the disciples privately,   saying,    Tell  us,   when
5023    2071  2532 5101 3588 4592    3588 4674   3952    2532 3588
ταῦτα ἔσται, καὶ τί τὸ σημεῖον τῆς σῆς παρουσίας, καὶ τῆς
these things will be, and what (is) the sign  of  your coming,    and of the
4930       3588 165     2532  611    3588 2424  2036   846
συντελείας τοῦ αἰῶνος. 4 καὶ ἀποκριθεὶς ὁ Ἰησοῦς εἶπεν αὐτοῖς,
termination of the age?   And answering   Jesus   said  to them
911     3361 5100 5209  4105       4183 1063 2064    1909
Βλέπετε, μή τις ὑμᾶς πλανήσῃ. 5 πολλοὶ γὰρ ἐλεύσονται ἐπὶ
See (that) not any of you misleads.   many  For  will come  on
3588 3686    3450   3004     1473 1510 3588 5547    2532 4183
τῷ ὀνόματί μου, λέγοντες, Ἐγώ εἰμι ὁ Χριστός· καὶ πολλοὺς
the name   of Me, saying,    I  am the Christ,   and  many
```

3. And He was sitting on the Mount of Olives, the disciples came to Him privately, saying, Tell us, when will these things be? And, What (is) the sign of Your coming and of the end of the age?

4 And answering, Jesus said to them, See (that) not any misleads you.

5 For many will come in My name, saying, I am the Christ, and

Matthew 24

1. And Jesus went out, and departed from the temple: and his disciples came to (him) for to show him the buildings of the temple.

2 And Jesus said unto them, See ye not all these things? Verily I say unto you, There shall not be left here one stone upon another, that shall not be thrown down.

3. And as he sat upon the mount of Olives, the disciples came unto him privately, saying, Tell us, when shall these things be? and what (shall be) the sign of thy coming, and of the end of the world?

4 And Jesus answered and said unto them, Take heed that no man deceive you.

5 For many shall come in my name, saying, I am Christ; and

Literal Translation	Matthew 24:6	King James Version

4105   3195   1161   191   4171   2532   189

(they) will cause many πλανήσουσι. 6 μελλήσετε δὲ ἀκούειν πολέμους καὶ ἀκοὰς shall deceive many.
to err   will cause to err   you are going But to hear of wars and rumors

6 But you are going to hear of wars and rumors of wars. See, do not be terrified. For all things must happen, but the end is not yet.

4171   3708 3361 2360   1163 1063 3956   1096   235

πολέμων· ὁρᾶτε, μὴ θροεῖσθε· δεῖ γὰρ πάντα γενέσθαι· ἀλλ'
of wars. See, not do be not terrified; must for all these things happen But

6 And ye shall hear of wars and rumours of wars: see that ye be not troubled: for all (these things) must come to pass, but the end is not yet.

3768 2076 3588 5056   1453   1063 1484 1909 1484 2532

οὔπω ἐστὶ τὸ τέλος. 7 ἐγερθήσεται γὰρ ἔθνος ἐπὶ ἔθνος, καὶ
not yet is the end will be raised For nation against nation, and

7 For nation will be raised against nation, and kingdom against kingdom; and there will be famines and plagues and earthquakes against (many) places.

932   1909 932   2532   2071 3042 2532 3061 2532

βασιλεία ἐπὶ βασιλείαν· καὶ ἔσονται λιμοὶ καὶ λοιμοὶ καὶ
kingdom against kingdom, and there will be famines and plagues and

7 For nation shall rise against nation, and kingdom against kingdom: and there shall be famines, and pestilences, and earthquakes, in divers places.

4578   2596 5117   3956 1161 5023 746   5604   5119

σεισμοὶ κατὰ τόπους. 8 πάντα δὲ ταῦτα ἀρχὴ ὠδίνων. 9 τότε
earthquakes against places. all But these (are) beginning of throes. Then

8 But all these (are) a beginning of throes.

9 Then they will deliver you up to affliction, and will kill you, and you will be hated by all nations because of My name.

3860   5209 1519 2347 2532   615   5209 2532

παραδώσουσιν ὑμᾶς εἰς θλίψιν, καὶ ἀποκτενοῦσιν ὑμᾶς· καὶ
they will deliver up you to affliction, and will kill   you and

8 All these (are) the beginning of sorrows.

9 Then shall they deliver you up to be afflicted, and shall kill you: and ye shall be hated of all nations for my name's sake.

2071   3404   5259 3956 3588 1484 1223 3588 3686 3450

ἔσεσθε μισούμενοι ὑπὸ πάντων τῶν ἐθνῶν διὰ τὸ ὄνομά μου.
you will be hated by all the nations because of name My.

2532 5119   4624   4183 2532 240   3860

10 And then many will be ensnared, and they will deliver up one another and will hate one another.

10 καὶ τότε σκανδαλισθήσονται πολλοί, καὶ ἀλλήλους παραδώ-
And then will be ensnared   many, and one another will deliver

10 And then shall many be offended, and shall betray one another, and shall hate one another.

2532   3404   240   2532 4183   5578

σουσι, καὶ μισήσουσιν ἀλλήλους· 11 καὶ πολλοὶ ψευδοπρο-
up. and they will hate one another. And many false

11 And many false prophets will be raised and will cause many to err.

1453   2532 4105   4183   2532 1223 3588

φῆται ἐγερθήσονται, καὶ πλανήσουσι πολλούς. 12 καὶ διὰ τὸ
prophets will be raised up, and will cause to err many. And because

11 And many false prophets shall rise, and shall deceive many.

12 And because lawlessness shall have been multiplied, the love of the many will grow cold.

4129   3588 458   5594   3588 26   3588

πληθυνθῆναι τὴν ἀνομίαν, ψυγήσεται ἡ ἀγάπη τῶν
will have been the lawlessness, will grow cold the love of the

12 And because iniquity shall abound, the love of many shall wax cold.

4183 3588 1161 5278   1519 5056 3278 4982   2532

πολλῶν· 13 ὁ δὲ ὑπομείνας εἰς τέλος, οὗτος σωθήσεται. 14 καὶ
many. the (one) But enduring to (the) end, this one will be kept safe. And

13 But he (the one) who endures to (the) end, that one will be kept safe.

13 But he that shall endure unto the end, the same shall be saved.

2784   5124 3588 2098   3588 932   1722 3650

κηρυχθήσεται τοῦτο τὸ εὐαγγέλιον τῆς βασιλείας ἐν ὅλῃ
will be proclaimed this   gospel of the kingdom in all

14 And this gospel of the Kingdom shall be preached in all the earth for a testimony to all the nations, and then will come the end.

3588 3625   1519 3142   3956 3588 1484 2532 5119   2240

τῇ οἰκουμένῃ εἰς μαρτύριον πᾶσι τοῖς ἔθνεσι· καὶ τότε ἥξει
the inhabited earth for a testimony to all the nations, and then will come

14 And this gospel of the kingdom shall be preached in all the world for a witness unto all nations; and then shall the end come.

3588 5056

τὸ τέλος.
the end.

15 Then when you see the abomination of desolation, which was spoken of by Daniel the prophet, standing in (the) holy place (the one) reading, let him understand),

3752 3767 1492 3588 946   3588   2050 3588 4483 1223

15.Ὅταν οὖν ἴδητε τὸ βδέλυγμα τῆς ἐρημώσεως τὸ ῥηθὲν διὰ
When, therefore you see the abomination of desolation   spoken through

15 When ye therefore shall see the abomination of desolation, spoken of by Daniel the prophet, stand in the holy place, (whoso readeth, let him understand:)

1158 3588 4396   2476 1722 5117 40 3588 314

Δανιὴλ τοῦ προφήτου, ἑστὼς ἐν τόπῳ ἁγίῳ ὁ ἀναγινώ-
Daniel the prophet, standing in place (the) holy (the one) reading

16 then let those in Judea flee into the mountains;

3539   5119 3588 1722 3588 2449   5343   1909

σκων νοείτω), 16 τότε οἱ ἐν τῇ Ἰουδαίᾳ φευγέτωσαν εἰς
let him understand, then the (ones) in Judea, let them flee into

16 Then let them which be in Judaea flee into the mountains:

17 the (one) on the housetop, let him not go down to take anything out of his house;

3588 3735 3588/1909/3588 1430 3361   2597   142 5100 1537

τὰ ὄρη· 17 ὁ ἐπὶ τοῦ δώματος μὴ καταβαινέτω ἆραι τι ἐκ
mountains, he on the housetops not let him go down to take anything from

17 Let him which is on the housetop not come down to take any thing out of his house:

18 and the (one) in the field, let him not turn back to take his garment.

3588 3614 846 2532/3588/1722/3588/68 3361 1994 2594

τῆς οἰκίας αὐτοῦ, 18 καὶ ὁ ἐν τῷ ἀγρῷ μὴ ἐπιστρεψάτω ὀπίσω
the house of him. And he in the field not let him turn behind

18 Neither let him which is in the field return back to take his clothes.

19 But woe to the (ones) having (a child) in (the) womb, and

142 3588 2440 846   3759 1161 3588 1722 1064 2192   2532

ἆραι τὰ ἱμάτια αὐτοῦ. 19 οὐαὶ δὲ ταῖς ἐν γαστρὶ ἐχούσαις καὶ
to take the garment of him woe And to the (ones) in womb having, and

19 And woe unto them that are with child, and

Literal Translation	Matthew 24:20	King James Version

to those suckling in those days!
20 And pray that your flight will not be in winter nor in a sabbath

3588 2337 1722 1565 3588 2250 4336 1161
ταῖς θηλαζούσαις ἐν ἐκείναις ταῖς ἡμέραις. 20προσεύχεσθε δὲ
to the (ones) suckling in those days. pray And
2443 3361 1096 3588 5437 5216 5494 3366 1722 4521
ἵνα μὴ γένηται ἡ φυγὴ ὑμῶν χειμῶνος, μηδὲ ἐν σαββάτῳ.
that not will occur the flight of you of winter, nor in a sabbath

to them that give suck in those days!
20 But pray ye that your flight be not in the winter, neither on the sabbath day:

21 For there will be great affliction, such as has not happened from (the) beginning of (the) world until now, no, nor ever will be.

2071 1063 5119 2347 3173 3634 3756 1096 575 746
21 Ἔσται γὰρ τότε θλίψις μεγάλη, οἵα οὐ γέγονεν ἀπ' ἀρχῆς
will be For then affliction great, such as not has occurred from (the) beginning
2889 2193 3588 3568 3761 3756 3361 1096 2532 1487 3361 2856
κόσμου ἕως τοῦ νῦν, οὐδ' οὐ μὴ γένηται. 22 καὶ εἰ μὴ ἐκολοβώ-
of world until now, neither never never occur. And except were cut

21 For then shall be great tribulation, such as was not since the beginning of the world to this time, no, nor ever shall be.

22 And except those days were shortened, not any flesh would be saved. But on account of the elect, those days will be shortened.

3588 2250 1565 3756 302 4982 3956 4561 1223 1161
θησαν αἱ ἡμέραι ἐκεῖναι, οὐκ ἂν ἐσώθη πᾶσα σάρξ· διὰ δὲ
short days those not would be saved any flesh; because of but
3588 1588 2856 3588 2250 1565 5119 1437
τοὺς ἐκλεκτοὺς κολοβωθήσονται αἱ ἡμέραι ἐκεῖναι. 23τότε ἐὰν
the elect will be cut short days those Then if

22 And except those days should be shortened, there should no flesh be saved: but for the elect's sake those days shall be shortened.

23 Then if anyone says to you, Behold, here (is) the Christ! Or, Here! Do not believe.

5100 5213 2036 2400 5602 3588 5547 2228 5602 3361 4100
τις ὑμῖν εἴπῃ, Ἰδού, ὧδε ὁ Χριστός, ἤ, Ὧδε· μὴ πιστεύσητε.
anyone of you says, Behold, here the Christ, or, Here; not do believe

23 Then if any man shall say unto you, Lo, here (is) Christ, or there; believe (it) not.

24 For false christs and false prophets will rise up And (they) will give great signs and wonders, so as to cause to err, if possible, even the elect
25 Behold, I tell you beforehand.

1453 1063 5580 2532 5578 2532
24 ἐγερθήσονται γὰρ ψευδόχριστοι καὶ ψευδοπροφῆται, καὶ
will rise up For false christs and false prophets, and
1325 4592 3173 2532 5059 5620 4105 1487
δώσουσι σημεῖα μεγάλα καὶ τέρατα, ὥστε πλανῆσαι, εἰ
they will give signs great and wonders, so as to cause to err, if
1415 2532 3588 1588 2400 4280 5213 1437 3767
δυνατόν, καὶ τοὺς ἐκλεκτούς. 25 Ἰδού, προείρηκα ὑμῖν. 26 ἐὰν οὖν
possible, even the elect. Behold, I have before told you. If, then,

24 For there shall arise false Christs, and false prophets, and shall shew great signs and wonders; insomuch that, if (it were) possible, they shall deceive the very elect.
25 Behold, I have told you before.

26 Then if they say to you, Behold, (He is) in the deserted (place), do not go out. Behold, (He is) in the inner rooms; do not believe.

2036 5213 2400 1722 3588 2048 2076 3361 1831 2400
εἴπωσιν ὑμῖν, Ἰδού, ἐν τῇ ἐρήμῳ ἐστί, μὴ ἐξέλθητε· Ἰδού,
they say to you, Behold, in the deserted He is! Not do go forth, behold, (place)
1722 3588 5009 3361 4100 5618 1063 3588 796
ἐν τοῖς ταμείοις, μὴ πιστεύσητε. 27 ὥσπερ γὰρ ἡ ἀστραπὴ
in the private rooms! Not do believe. as For the lightning

26 Wherefore if they shall say unto you, Behold, he is in the desert; go not forth: behold, (he is) in the secret chambers; believe (it) not.

27 For as the lightning comes forth from (the) east and shines as far as (the) west, so also will be the coming of the Son of man.

1831 575 395 2532 5316 2193 1424 3779
ἐξέρχεται ἀπὸ ἀνατολῶν καὶ φαίνεται ἕως δυσμῶν, οὕτως
comes forth from (the) east and shines as far as (the) west, so
2071 2532 3588 3952 3588 5207 3588 444 3699 1063
ἔσται καὶ ἡ παρουσία τοῦ υἱοῦ τοῦ ἀνθρώπου. 28 ὅπου γὰρ
will be also the coming of the Son of man. wherever For

27 For as the lightning cometh out of the east, and shineth even unto the west; so shall also the coming of the Son of man be.

28 For wherever the dead body may be, there the eagles will be gathered.

1437 5600 3588 4430 1563 4863 3588 105
ἐὰν ᾖ τὸ πτῶμα, ἐκεῖ συναχθήσονται οἱ ἀετοί.
if may be the carcase, there will be gathered the eagles

28 For wheresoever the carcase is, there will the eagles be gathered together.

29. And immediately after the affliction of those days the sun will be darkened and the moon will not give her light, and the stars will fall from the heaven, and the powers of the heavens will be shaken.

2112 1161 3326 3588 2347 3588 2250 1565 3588 2246
29. Εὐθέως δὲ μετὰ τὴν θλίψιν τῶν ἡμερῶν ἐκείνων, ὁ ἥλιος
Immediately And after the affliction of days those, the sun
4654 2532 3588 4582 3756 1325 3588 5338 846
σκοτισθήσεται, καὶ ἡ σελήνη οὐ δώσει τὸ φέγγος αὐτῆς,
will be darkened, and the moon not will give the light of her,
2532 3588 792 4098 575 3588 3772 2532 3588 1411
καὶ οἱ ἀστέρες πεσοῦνται ἀπὸ τοῦ οὐρανοῦ, καὶ αἱ δυνάμεις
and the stars will fall from the heaven, and the powers

29. Immediately after the tribulation of those days shall the sun be darkened, and the moon shall not give her light, and the stars shall fall from heaven, and the powers of the heavens shall be shaken:

30 And then the sign of the Son of man will appear in the heavens. And then all the tribes of the land will wail. And they will see the Son

3588 3772 4531 2532 5119 5316 3588
τῶν οὐρανῶν σαλευθήσονται. 30 καὶ τότε φανήσεται τὸ
of the heavens will be shaken And then will appear the
4592 3588 5207 3588 444 1722 3588 3772 2532 5119
σημεῖον τοῦ υἱοῦ τοῦ ἀνθρώπου ἐν τῷ οὐρανῷ· καὶ τότε
sign of the Son of man in the heavens, and then
2875 3956 3588 5443 3588 1093 2532 3700 3588 5207 3588
κόψονται πᾶσαι αἱ φυλαὶ τῆς γῆς, καὶ ὄψονται τὸν υἱὸν τοῦ
will wail all the tribes of the land, and they will see the Son

30 And then shall appear the sign of the Son of man in heaven: and then shall all the tribes of the earth mourn, and they shall see the Son

of man coming on the
clouds of heaven with
power and much glory.
(Dan. 7:13)
31 And He will send His
angels with a great
sound of a trumpet, and
they will gather His
elect from the four
winds, from the ends of
(the) heavens to their
ends.

444   2064   1909 3588   3507   3588   3772   3326
ἀνθρώπου ἐρχόμενον ἐπὶ τῶν νεφελῶν τοῦ οὐρανοῦ μετὰ
of man   coming   on   the   clouds   of heaven   with

1411   2532   1391   4183   2532   649   3588   32
δυνάμεως καὶ δόξης πολλῆς. 31 καὶ ἀποστελεῖ τοὺς ἀγγέλους
power   and   glory   much.   And He will send   the   angels

846   3326   4536   5456   3173   2532   1996
αὐτοῦ μετὰ σάλπιγγος φωνῆς μεγάλης, καὶ ἐπισυνάξουσι
of Him   with   of a trumpet   sound   a great,   and   they will gather

3588   1588   846   1537 3588   5064   417   575   206
τοὺς ἐκλεκτοὺς αὐτοῦ ἐκ τῶν τεσσάρων, ἀνέμων, ἀπ' ἄκρων
the   elect   of Him out of the four   winds,   from   (the) ends

3772   2193   206   846
οὐρανῶν· ἕως ἄκρων αὐτῶν.
of (the) heavens to (the) ends of them.

of man coming in the
clouds of heaven with
power and great glory.

31 And he shall send his
angels with a great
sound of a trumpet, and
they shall gather to-
gether his elect from the
four winds, from one
end of heaven to the
other.

32. But learn the par-
able from the fig-tree:
When its tender shoot
becomes tender and it
puts out leaves, you
know that the summer
(is) near;
33 so also you, when
you see all these things,
know that it is near at
(the) doors.
34 Truly I say to you. In
no way will this genera-
tion pass away until all
these things shall occur

575   1161 3588   4808   3129   3588   3850   3752 2235 3588
32. Ἀπὸ δὲ τῆς συκῆς μάθετε τὴν παραβολήν· ὅταν ἤδη ὁ
from And the   fig-tree   learn   the   parable: When   now the

2798   846   1096   527   2532 3588   5444   1631   1097
κλάδος αὐτῆς γένηται ἁπαλὸς καὶ τὰ φύλλα ἐκφύῃ, γινώ-
tender shoot of it   becomes   tender,   and   the   leaves it puts out   you

3754 1451 3588 2330   3779 2532 5210 3752 1492   3956
σκετε ὅτι ἐγγὺς τὸ θέρος· 33 οὕτω καὶ ὑμεῖς, ὅταν ἴδητε πάντα
know that near (is) the summer;   so   also you   when you see   all

5023   1097   3754 1451   2076 1909 2374   281   3004
ταῦτα, γινώσκετε ὅτι ἐγγύς ἐστιν ἐπὶ θύραις. 34 ἀμὴν λέγω
these things know   that   near   it is   on (the) doors   Truly I say

5213   3756 3361   3928   3588   1074   3778 2193 302 3956   5023
ὑμῖν, οὐ μὴ παρέλθῃ ἡ γενεὰ αὕτη, ἕως ἂν πάντα ταῦτα
to you, not at all passes away   generation this   until should all these things

1096   3588 3772   2532 3588 1093 3928   3588 1161 3056
γένηται. 35 ὁ οὐρανὸς καὶ ἡ γῆ παρελεύσεται, οἱ δὲ λόγοι
occur.   The   heavens   and the earth will pass away,   the but words

32. Now learn a par-
able of the fig tree;
When his branch is yet
tender, and putteth forth
leaves, ye know that
summer (is) nigh:

33 So likewise ye, when
ye shall see all these
things, know that it is
near, (even) at the
doors.
34 Verily I say unto you,
This generation shall
not pass, till all these
things be fulfilled.

35 The heaven and the
earth will pass away; but
not My words will pass
away, never.
36. But as to that day
and that hour, no one
knows, neither the an-
gels of Heaven, except
My Father only.

3450 3756 3361   3928   4012 1161 3588   2250   1565   2532 3588
μου οὐ μὴ παρέλθωσι. 36 περὶ δὲ τῆς ἡμέρας ἐκείνης καὶ τῆς
of Me not never will pass away.   about But   day   that   and   the

5610   3762   1492   3761 3588   32   3588 3772   1487 3361 3588
ὥρας οὐδεὶς οἶδεν, οὐδὲ οἱ ἄγγελοι τῶν οὐρανῶν, εἰ μὴ ὁ
hour   no one   knows,   neither the   angels   of the heavens,   except the

3962   3450   3441   5618   1161 3588   2250   3588 3575   3779
πατήρ μου μόνος. 37 ὥσπερ δὲ αἱ ἡμέραι τοῦ Νῶε, οὕτως
Father of Me only.   as   But the   days   of Noah,   so

2071   2532 3588   3952   3588 5207   3588   444   5618   1063
ἔσται καὶ ἡ παρουσία τοῦ υἱοῦ τοῦ ἀνθρώπου. 38 ὥσπερ γὰρ
will be also the   coming   of the Son   of man.   as   For

35 Heaven and earth
shall pass away, but my
words shall not pass
away.
36. But of that day and
hour knoweth no (man),
no, not the angels of
heaven, but my Father
only.

37 But as the days of
Noah, so also will be the
coming of the Son of
man.
38 For as they were in
the days before the
flood: eating, and drink-
ing, marrying, and giv-
ing in marriage, until
(the) day (when) Noah
went into the ark.

2258   1722 3588   2250   3588 4253 3588   2627   5176
ἦσαν ἐν ταῖς ἡμέραις ταῖς πρὸ τοῦ κατακλυσμοῦ τρώγοντες
they were in the   days   before the   flood,   eating,

2532   4095   1060   2532   1547   891 3739 2250
καὶ πίνοντες, γαμοῦντες καὶ ἐκγαμίζοντες, ἄχρι ἧς ἡμέρας
and   drinking,   marrying   and giving in marriage, until which   day

37 But as the days of
Noe (were), so shall
also the coming of the
Son of man be.
38 For as in the days that
were before the flood
they were eating and
drinking, marrying and
giving in marriage, until
the day that Noe entered
into the ark,

39 And they did not
know until the flood
came and took all away.
So also will be the com-
ing of the Son of man.

1525   3575   1519 3588   2787   2532 3756   1097   2193 2064
εἰσῆλθε Νῶε εἰς τὴν κιβωτόν, 39 καὶ οὐκ ἔγνωσαν, ἕως ἦλθεν
entered   Noah into the   ark,   and not (they)knew until   came

3588   2627   2532   142   537   3779   2071 2532 3588 3952
ὁ κατακλυσμὸς καὶ ἦρεν ἅπαντας, οὕτως ἔσται καὶ ἡ παρου-
the   flood   and took   all,   so   will be   the coming

39 And knew not until
the flood came, and
took them all away; so
shall also the coming of
the Son of man be.

40 Then two will be out
in the field; the one is
taken away, and the one
is left;
41 two grinding in

3588 5207   3588   444   5119 1417   2071   1722 3588   68
σία τοῦ υἱοῦ τοῦ ἀνθρώπου. 40 τότε δύο ἔσονται ἐν τῷ ἀγρῷ·
of the Son   of man.   Then two will be   in the field,

3588 1520   3880   2532/3588/1520   863   1417   229   1722
ὁ εἷς παραλαμβάνεται, καὶ ὁ εἷς ἀφίεται. 41 δύο ἀλήθουσαι ἐν
the one   is taken away,   and the one   is left;   two   grinding   in

40 Then shall two be in
the field; the one shall
be taken, and the other
left.
41 Two (women shall
be) grinding at

Matthew 24:42

Literal Translation

the mill; one is taken away, and one is left.
42. Watch, then, because you do not know in what hour your Lord comes

43 But know this, that if the housemaster had known in what watch the thief is coming, he would have watched and not have allowed his house to be dug through.
44 Because of this, you also be ready, for in that hour you think not, the Son of man comes

45 Who then is the faithful and prudent servant whom his lord has set over his care, to give to them the food in season?

46 Blessed (is) that servant whom his lord shall find so doing when he comes.
47 Truly I say to you, He will set him over all his substance

48 But if that bad servant says in his heart. My lord delays to come, 49 and begins to beat (his) fellow servants, and to eat and to drink with the (ones) drinking.

50 the lord of that slave will come in a day in which he does not expect and in an hour which he does not know,
51 and will cut him in two, and will appoint his portion with the hypocrites. There will be weeping and gnashing of the teeth.

Greek (interlinear)

3588 3459 | 3391 | 3880 | 2532 3391 863 | 1127
τῷ μύλωνι μία παραλαμβάνεται καὶ μία ἀφίεται. 42 γρηγο-
the mill one is taken away and one is left Watch

3767 3754 3756 1492 4169 5610 3588 2962 5216 2064
ρεῖτε οὖν, ὅτι οὐκ οἴδατε ποίᾳ ὥρᾳ ὁ Κύριος ὑμῶν ἔρχεται.
then because not you know on what hour the Lord of you is coming.

1565 1161 1097 3754 1487 1492 3588 3617 4169
43 ἐκεῖνο δὲ γινώσκετε, ὅτι εἰ ᾔδει ὁ οἰκοδεσπότης ποίᾳ
this And know, that if knew the housemaster in what

5438 3588 2812 2064 1127 302 2532 3756 302 1439
φυλακῇ ὁ κλέπτης ἔρχεται, ἐγρηγόρησεν ἄν, καὶ οὐκ ἄν εἴασε
watch the thief is coming, he would have watched and not might allow

1358 3588 3614 846 1223 5124 2532 5210 1096
διορυγῆναι τὴν οἰκίαν αὐτοῦ. 44 διὰ τοῦτο καὶ ὑμεῖς γίνεσθε
to be dug through the house of him. Because of this also you become

2092 3754 3739 5610 3756 1380 3588 5207 3588 444 2064
ἕτοιμοι· ὅτι ᾗ ὥρᾳ οὐ δοκεῖτε, ὁ υἱὸς τοῦ ἀνθρώπου ἔρχεται.
ready; because that hour not you think, the Son of man comes

5101 687 2076 3588 4103 1401 2532 5429 3739 2525
45 τίς ἄρα ἐστὶν ὁ πιστὸς δοῦλος καὶ φρόνιμος, ὃν κατέστησεν
Who then is the faithful slave and prudent, whom appointed

3588 2962 846 1909 3588 2322 846 3588 1325
ὁ κύριος αὐτοῦ ἐπὶ τῇ θεραπείας αὐτοῦ, τοῦ διδόναι
the lord of him over the care of him, to give

846 3588 5160 1722 2540 3107 3588 1401 1565 3739
αὐτοῖς τὴν τροφὴν ἐν καιρῷ; 46 μακάριος ὁ δοῦλος ἐκεῖνος, ὃν
to them the food in season? Blessed (is) slave that whom

2064 3588 2962 846 2147 4160 3779 281 3004
ἐλθὼν ὁ κύριος αὐτοῦ εὑρήσει ποιοῦντα οὕτως. 47 ἀμὴν λέγω
coming the lord of him will find doing so Truly I say

5213 3754 1909 3956 3588 5224 846 2525
ὑμῖν, ὅτι ἐπὶ πᾶσι τοῖς ὑπάρχουσιν αὐτοῦ καταστήσει
to you that over all the substance of him he will appoint

846 1437 1161 2036 3588 2556 1401 1565 1722 3588 2588
αὐτόν. 48 ἐὰν δὲ εἴπῃ ὁ κακὸς δοῦλος ἐκεῖνος ἐν τῇ καρδίᾳ
him if But says bad slave that in the heart

846 5549 3588 2962 3450 2064 2532 756 5180
αὐτοῦ, Χρονίζει ὁ κύριός μου ἐλθεῖν, 49 καὶ ἄρξηται τύπτειν
of him delays the lord of me to come, and should begin to beat

3588 4889 2068 1161 2532 4095 3326 3588 3184
τοὺς συνδούλους, ἐσθίειν δὲ καὶ πίνειν μετὰ τῶν μεθυόντων,
the fellow-slaves, to eat and also to drink with the (ones) drinking.

2240 3588 2962 3588 1401 1565 1161 2250 3739 3756
50 ἥξει ὁ κύριος τοῦ δούλου ἐκείνου ἐν ἡμέρᾳ ᾗ οὐ
comes the lord of that slave in a day which not

4328 2532 1722 5610 3739 3756 1097 2532 1371
προσδοκᾷ, καὶ ἐν ὥρᾳ ᾗ οὐ γινώσκει, 51 καὶ διχοτομήσει
he expects and in an hour which not he knows, and will cut in two

846 2532 3588 3313 846 3326 3588 5273 5087 1563
αὐτόν, καὶ τὸ μέρος αὐτοῦ μετὰ τῶν ὑποκριτῶν θήσει· ἐκεῖ
him, and the portion of him with the hypocrites will put. There

2071 3588 2805 2532 3588 1030 3588 3599
ἔσται ὁ κλαυθμὸς καὶ ὁ βρυγμὸς τῶν ὀδόντων.
will be the weeping and the gnashing of the teeth.

King James Version

the mill; the one shall be taken, and the other left.
42. Watch therefore: for ye know not what hour your Lord doth come.

43 But know this, that if the goodman of the house had known in what watch the thief would come, he would have watched, and would not have suffered his house to be broken up.
44 Therefore be ye also ready: for in such an hour as ye think not the Son of man cometh.

45 Who then is a faithful and wise servant, whom his lord hath made ruler over his household, to give them meat in due season?

46 Blessed (is) that servant, whom his lord when he cometh shall find so doing.
47 Verily I say unto you, That he shall make him ruler over all his goods.

48 But and if that evil servant shall say in his heart, My lord delayeth his coming;
49 And shall begin to smite (his) fellowservants, and to eat and drink with the drunken;

50 The lord of that servant shall come in a day when he looketh not for (him), and in an hour that he is not aware of,
51 And shall cut him asunder, and appoint (him) his portion with the hypocrites: there shall be weeping and gnashing of teeth.

Acrostic Index

The following is the full chapter, in English and in Greek of Mark: Chapter 8, Verse 34, where acrostic 3 begins, is clearly marked.

1. The crowd being very great in those days, and not having anything they may eat, Jesus, having called near His disciples, said to them,

2 I have pity on the crowd because now three days they continue with Me, and they do not have what they may eat.

3 And if I send them away fasting to their house, they will faint in the way, for some of them come from afar.

4 And His disciples answered Him. From where will anyone here be able to satisfy these (with) loaves in a deserted (place)?

5 And He asked them. How many loaves do you have? And they said. Seven.

```
      1722  1565    3588    2250        3827     3793   5607   2532
1. Ἐν ἐκείναις ταῖς ἡμέραις, παμπόλλου ὄχλου ὄντος, καὶ
    In    those            days,   very great  the crowd being, and

  3361   2192   5101  5315          4341          3588 2424    3588
  μὴ ἐχόντων τί φάγωσι, προσκαλεσάμενος ὁ Ἰησοῦς τοὺς
  not having anything they may eat, having called near   Jesus   the

  3101      846   3004    846        4697          1909 3588 3793
μαθητὰς αὐτοῦ λέγει αὐτοῖς, 2 Σπλαγχνίζομαι ἐπὶ τὸν ὄχλον·
disciples of Him He says to them,   I have pity     on the crowd,

 3754 2235  2250    5140      4357      3427 2532 3756  2192  5101
 ὅτι ἤδη ἡμέρας τρεῖς προσμένουσί μοι, καὶ οὐκ ἔχουσι τί
 because now days   three  they continue with Me, and not  have what

  5315       2532 1437  630      846       3523   1519 3624    846
 φάγωσι· 3 καὶ ἐὰν ἀπολύσω αὐτοὺς νήστεις εἰς οἶκον αὐτῶν,
 they may eat. And if  I send away  them   fasting to (the) house of them,

   1590          1722 3588 3598  5100  1063  846      3113     2240
 ἐκλυθήσονται ἐν τῇ ὁδῷ· τινὲς γὰρ αὐτῶν μακρόθεν ἥκασι.
 they will faint  in  the way;  some for of them  from afar  are come.

 2532   611          846 3588 3101    846       4159      5128
4 καὶ ἀπεκρίθησαν αὐτῷ οἱ μαθηταὶ αὐτοῦ, Πόθεν τούτους
  And  answered      Him the disciples of Him, From where these

  1410     5100 5602    5526     740   1909   2047       2532
 δυνήσεταί τις ὧδε χορτάσαι ἄρτων ἐπ᾽ ἐρημίας; 5 καὶ
 will be able anyone here to satisfy (with) loaves on a deserted (place), and

  1905    846      4214      2192   740  3588/1161/2036    2033
 ἐπηρώτα αὐτούς, Πόσους ἔχετε ἄρτους; οἱ δὲ εἶπον, Ἑπτά.
 He asked them,   How many have you loaves? they And said,  Seven.
```

---

1. In those days the multitude being very great, and having nothing to eat, Jesus called his disciples (unto him), and saith unto them,

2 I have compassion on the multitude, because they have now been with me three days, and have nothing to eat:

3 And if I send them away fasting to their own houses, they will faint by the way: for divers of them came from far.

4 And his disciples answered him, From whence can a man satisfy these (men) with bread here in the wilderness?

5 And he asked them, How many loaves have ye? And they said, Seven.

Literal Translation	Greek Text	King James Version
6 And He ordered the crowd to recline on the ground. And taking the seven loaves, giving thanks, He broke and gave to His disciples, that they might serve. And they served the crowd	2532 3853 3588 3793 377 1909 3588 1093 2532 2983 / 6 καὶ παρήγγειλε τῷ ὄχλῳ ἀναπεσεῖν ἐπὶ τῆς γῆς· καὶ λαβὼν / And He ordered the crowd to recline on the ground. And taking / 3588 2033 740 2168 2806 2532 1325 3588 / τοὺς ἑπτὰ ἄρτους, εὐχαριστήσας ἔκλασε καὶ ἐδίδου τοῖς / the seven loaves, having given thanks, He broke and gave to the / 3101 846 2443 3908 2532 3908 3588 3793 / μαθηταῖς αὐτοῦ, ἵνα παραθῶσι· καὶ παρέθηκαν τῷ ὄχλῳ. / disciples of Him, that they may serve. And they served the crowd	6 And he commanded the people to sit down on the ground: and he took the seven loaves, and gave thanks, and brake, and gave to his disciples to set before (them); and they did set (them) before the people.
7 And they had a few fish. And blessing, He said for these also to be served.	2532 2192 2485 3641 2532 2127 2036 3908 2532 / 7 καὶ εἶχον ἰχθύδια ὀλίγα· καὶ εὐλογήσας εἶπε παραθεῖναι καὶ / And they had fish a few. And having blessed He said to be served also	7 And they had a few small fishes: and he blessed, and commanded to set them also before (them).
8 And they ate, and were satisfied. And (they) took up over and above seven lunch baskets (of) fragments.	846 5315 1161 2532 5526 2532 142 4051 / αὐτά. ℵ Ἔφαγον δέ, καὶ ἐχορτάσθησαν· καὶ ἦραν περισσεύματα / these they ate And, and were satisfied, and took up over and above / 2801 2033 4711 2258 1161 3588 5315 5613 / κλασμάτων ἑπτὰ σπυρίδας. 9 ἦσαν δὲ οἱ φαγόντες ὡς / of fragments seven lunch-baskets. were And those eating about	8 So they did eat, and were filled: and they took up of the broken (meat) that was left seven baskets.
9 And those eating were about four thousand. And He sent them away.	5070 2532 630 846 2532 2112 1684 1519 / τετρακισχίλιοι· καὶ ἀπέλυσεν αὐτούς. 10 καὶ εὐθέως ἐμβὰς εἰς / four thousand; and He sent away them And at once entering into	9 And they that had eaten were about four thousand: and he sent them away.
10. And at once entering into the boat with His disciples, He came into the region of Dal-manutha.	3588 4143 3326 3588 3101 846 2064 1519 3588 3313 / τὸ πλοῖον μετὰ τῶν μαθητῶν αὐτοῦ, ἦλθεν εἰς τὰ μέρη / the boat with the disciples of Him, He came into the region / 1148 / Δαλμανουθά. / of Dalmanutha	10. And straightway he entered into a ship with his disciples, and came into the parts of Dalmanutha.
11 And the Pharisees went out and began to argue with Him, seeking from Him a sign from Heaven, tempting Him.	2532 1831 3588 5330 2532 756 4802 846 / 11. Καὶ ἐξῆλθον οἱ Φαρισαῖοι, καὶ ἤρξαντο συζητεῖν αὐτῷ, / And went out the Pharisees, and began to argue with Him, / 2212 3844 846 4592 575 3588 3772 3985 / ζητοῦντες παρ' αὐτοῦ σημεῖον ἀπὸ τοῦ οὐρανοῦς, πειρά- / seeking from Him a sign from Heaven, tempting	11 And the Pharisees came forth, and began to question with him, seeking of him a sign from heaven, tempting him.
12 And groaning in His spirit, He said, Why does this generation seek a sign? Truly I say to you, (As) if this generation will be given a sign!	846 2532 389 3588 4151 846 3004 / ζοντες αὐτόν. 12 καὶ ἀναστενάξας τῷ πνεύματι αὐτοῦ λέγει, / Him. And groaning in the spirit of Him He says, / 5101 3588 1074 3778 4592 1934 281 3004 5213 1487 / Τί ἡ γενεὰ αὕτη σημεῖον ἐπιζητεῖ; ἀμὴν λέγω ὑμῖν, εἰ / Why generation this a sign seeks? Truly I say to you, (As) if / 1325 3588 1074 3778 4592 2532 863 846 1684 / δοθήσεται τῇ γενεᾷ ταύτῃ σημεῖον. 13 καὶ ἀφεὶς αὐτούς, ἐμβὰς / will be given generation to this a sign! And leaving them, entering	12 And he sighed deeply in his spirit, and saith, Why doth this generation seek after a sign? verily I say unto you, There shall no sign be given unto this generation.
13 And leaving them, again entering into the boat, He went away to the other side.	3825 1519 3588 4143 565 1519 3588 4008 / πάλιν εἰς τὸ πλοῖον, ἀπῆλθεν εἰς τὸ πέραν. / again into the boat, He went away to the other side	13 And he left them, and entering into the ship again departed to the other side.
14. And the disciples forgot to take loaves. And they did not have (any) with themselves in the boat, except one loaf.	2532 1950 3588 3101 2983 740 2532 1487 3361 1520 / 14. Καὶ ἐπελάθοντο οἱ μαθηταὶ λαβεῖν ἄρτους, καὶ εἰ μὴ ἕνα / And forgot the disciples to take loaves. and except one / 740 3756 2192 3326 1438 1722 3588 4143 2532 1291 / ἄρτον οὐκ εἶχον μεθ' ἑαυτῶν ἐν τῷ πλοίῳ. 15 καὶ διεστέλλετο / loaf not they had with themselves in the boat. And he charged	14. Now (the disciples) had forgotten to take bread, neither had they in the ship with them more than one loaf.
15 And He charged them, saying, See! Look out from the leaven of the Pharisees, and of the leaven of Herod.	846 3004 3708 991 575 3588 2219 3588 / αὐτοῖς, λέγων, Ὁρᾶτε, βλέπετε ἀπὸ τῆς ζύμης τῶν / them, saying, See, look out from the leaven of the / 5330 2532 3588 2219 2264 2532 1260 4314 / Φαρισαίων καὶ τῆς ζύμης Ἡρώδου. 16 καὶ διελογίζοντο πρὸς / Pharisees and of the leaven of Herod. And they reasoned with	15 And he charged them, saying, Take heed, beware of the leaven of the Pharisees, and (of) the leaven of Herod.
16 And they reasoned with one another, saying. Because we have no loaves.	240 3004 1754 740 3756 2192 2532 1097 3588 / ἀλλήλους, λέγοντες, ὅτι Ἄρτους οὐκ ἔχομεν. 17 καὶ γνοὺς ὁ / one another, saying, Because loaves not we have. And knowing	16 And they reasoned among themselves, saying, (It is) because we have no bread.
17 And knowing, Jesus said to them, Why do you reason because you have no loaves?	2424 3004 846 5101 1260 3754 740 3756 2192 / Ἰησοῦς λέγει αὐτοῖς, Τί διαλογίζεσθε ὅτι ἄρτους οὐκ ἔχετε; / Jesus says to them, Why do you reason because loaves not you have?	17 And when Jesus knew (it), he saith unto them, Why reason ye because ye have no bread?

Literal Translation

Do you not yet perceive nor realize? Have you still hardened your heart?
18 Having eyes, do you not see? And having ears, do you not hear? And do you not remember? (Jer. 5:21)
19 When I broke the five loaves to the five thousand, how many hand-baskets full of fragments did you take up? They said to Him, Twelve.
20 And when the seven to the four thousand, how many lunch-baskets did you take up (with the) fillings of fragments? And they said, Seven.
21 And He said to them, How do you not understand?

Interlinear

3768 3339 3761 4920 2089 4456 2192 3588
οὔπω νοεῖτε, οὐδὲ συνίετε; ἔπι πεπωρωμένην ἔχετε τὴν
not yet Do you perceive, nor realize? still hardened have you the

2588 5216 3788 2192 3756 991 2532 3775
καρδίαν ὑμῶν; 18 ὀφθαλμοὺς ἔχοντες οὐ βλέπετε; καὶ ὦτα
heart of you? eyes Having not do you see? And ears

2192 3756 191 2532 3756 3421 3753 3588 4002
ἔχοντες οὐκ ἀκούετε; καὶ οὐ μνημονεύετε; 19 Ὅτε τοὺς πέντε
having not do you hear? And not do you remember? When the five

740 2806 1519 3588 4000 4214 2894
ἄρτους ἔκλασα εἰς τοὺς πεντακισχιλίους, πόσους κοφίνους
loaves I broke to the five thousand, how many hand-baskets

4134 2801 142 3004 846 1427 3753
πλήρεις κλασμάτων ἤρατε; λέγουσιν αὐτῷ, Δώδεκα. 20 Ὅτε
full of fragments you took up? They say to Him, Twelve. when

1161 3588 2033 1519 3588 5070 4214 4711
δὲ τοὺς ἑπτὰ εἰς τοὺς τετρακισχιλίους, πόσων σπυρίδων
And the seven to the four thousand, how many lunch-baskets

4138 2801 142 3588 1161 2036 2033 2532
πληρώματα κλασμάτων ἤρατε; οἱ δὲ εἶπον, Ἑπτά. 21 καὶ
(the) fillings of fragments you took up? they And said, Seven. And

3004 846 4459 3756 4920
ἔλεγεν αὐτοῖς, Πῶς οὐ συνίετε;
He said to them, How not do you understand?

2532 2064 1519 966 2532 5342 846 5185
22. Καὶ ἔρχεται εἰς Βηθσαϊδά. καὶ φέρουσιν αὐτῷ τυφλόν,
And He comes into Bethsaida And they carry to Him a blind one

2532 3870 846 2443 846 680 2532 1949
καὶ παρακαλοῦσιν αὐτὸν ἵνα αὐτοῦ ἅψηται. 23 καὶ ἐπιλαβό-
And they beg him that He would touch. And having taken

3588 5495 3588 5185 1806 846 1854 3588
μενος τῆς χειρὸς τοῦ τυφλοῦ, ἐξήγαγεν αὐτὸν ἔξω τῆς
hold of the hand of the blind one. He led forth him outside the

2968 2532 4429 1519 3588 3659 846 2007 1588 5495
κώμης· καὶ πτύσας εἰς τὰ ὄμματα αὐτοῦ, ἐπιθεὶς τὰς χεῖρας
village. And having spit into the eyes of him, having laid the hands

846 1905 846 1487 5100 991 2532 308 3004
αὐτῷ, ἐπηρώτα αὐτὸν εἴ τι βλέπει. 24 καὶ ἀναβλέψας ἔλεγε,
on him, He asked him if anything he sees? And having looked he said,

991 3588 444 5613 1186 4043 1534
Βλέπω τοὺς ἀνθρώπους ὡς δένδρα περιπατοῦντας. 25 εἶτα
I see men as trees walking around. Then

3825 2007 3588 5495 1909 3588 3788 846 2532
πάλιν ἐπέθηκε τὰς χεῖρας ἐπὶ τοὺς ὀφθαλμοὺς αὐτοῦ, καὶ
again He placed the hands on the eyes of him, and

4160 846 308 2532 600 2532 1689
ἐποίησεν αὐτὸν ἀναβλέψαι, καὶ ἀποκατεστάθη, καὶ ἐνέβλεψε
made him look up. And he was restored, and saw

5081 537 2532 649 846 1519 3588 3624
τηλαυγῶς ἅπαντας. 26 καὶ ἀπέστειλεν αὐτὸν εἰς τὸν οἶκον
clearly all And He sent him to the house

846 3004 3366 1519 3588 2968 1525 3366 2036
αὐτοῦ, λέγων, Μηδὲ εἰς τὴν κώμην εἰσέλθῃς, μηδὲ εἴπῃς
of him, saying, Not into the village you may go in, nor may tell

5100 1722 3588 2968
τινὶ ἐν τῇ κώμῃ.
anyone in the village.

2532 1831 3588 2424 2532 3588 3101 846 1519 3588
27. Καὶ ἐξῆλθεν ὁ Ἰησοῦς καὶ οἱ μαθηταὶ αὐτοῦ εἰς τὰς
And went out Jesus and the disciples of Him into the

2968 2542 3588 5376 2532/1722/3588/3598 1905
κώμας Καισαρείας τῆς Φιλίππου· καὶ ἐν τῇ ὁδῷ ἐπηρώτα
villages of Caesarea of Philip And in the way He questioned

22. And He came to Bethsaida. And they carried a blind one to Him, and they beg Him that He would touch him.
23 And having taken hold of the blind one's hand, He led him forth outside the village. And spitting into his eyes, having laid (His) hands on him, He asked him if he sees anything.
24 And having looked, he said, I see men as trees walking.
25 Then again He placed (His) hands on his eyes again, and made him look up. And he was restored and saw all clearly.
26 And He sent him to his house, saying, You may not go into the village, nor may tell anyone in the village.
27. And Jesus and His disciples went out to the villages of Caesarea of Philip. And in the way, He questioned

King James Version

perceive ye not yet, neither understand? have ye your heart yet hardened?
18 Having eyes, see ye not? and having ears, hear ye not? and do ye not remember?
19 When I brake the five loaves among five thousand, how many baskets full of fragments took ye up? They say unto him, Twelve.
20 And when the seven among four thousand, how many baskets full of fragments took ye up? And they said, Seven.
21 And he said unto them, How is it that ye do not understand?
22. And he cometh to Bethsaida; and they bring a blind man unto him, and besought him to touch him.
23 And he took the blind man by the hand, and led him out of the town; and when he had spit on his eyes, and put his hands upon him, he asked him if he saw ought.
24 And he looked up, and said, I see men as trees, walking.
25 After that he put (his) hands again upon his eyes, and made him look up: and he was restored, and saw every man clearly.
26 And he sent him away to his house, saying, Neither go into the town, nor tell (it) to any in the town.
27. And Jesus went out, and his disciples, into the towns of Caesarea Philippi: and by the way he asked

His disciples, saying to them; Whom do men say Me to be?

3588 3101 846 3004 846 5101 3165 3004 3588
τοὺς μαθητὰς αὐτοῦ, λέγων αὐτοῖς, Τίνα με λέγουσιν οἱ
the disciples of Him, saying to them, Whom Me say

his disciples, saying unto them, Whom do men say that I am?

28 And they answered, John the Baptist, and others (say) Elijah; but others, one of the prophets.

444 1511 3588 1161 611 2491 3588 910
ἄνθρωποι εἶναι; 28 οἱ δὲ ἀπεκρίθησαν, Ἰωάννην τὸν βαπτι-
men to be? they And answered, John the Baptist;

2532 243 2243 243 1161 1520 3588 4396 2532
στήν· καὶ ἄλλοι, Ἡλίαν, ἄλλοι δὲ ἕνα τῶν προφητῶν 29 καὶ
and others, Elijah, others but one of the prophets. And

28 And they answered, John the Baptist: but some (say), Elias; and others, One of the prophets.

29 And He said to them, And you, whom do you say Me to be? And answering, Peter said to Him, You are the Christ.

846 3004 846 5210 1161 5101 3165 3004 1511 611
αὐτὸς λέγει αὐτοῖς, Ὑμεῖς δὲ τίνα με λέγετε εἶναι; ἀποκριθεὶς
He says to them, you And whom Me say you to be? answering

1161 3588 4074 3004 846 4771 1488 3588 5547 2532 2008
δὲ ὁ Πέτρος λέγει αὐτῷ, Σὺ εἶ ὁ Χριστός. 30 καὶ ἐπετίμησεν
And Peter says to Him, You are the Christ! And He warned

29 And he saith unto them, But whom say ye that I am? And Peter answereth and saith unto him, Thou art the Christ.

30 And He warned them that they may tell no one about Him.

846 2443 3367 3004 4012 846 2532 756 1321
αὐτοῖς, ἵνα μηδενὶ λέγωσι περὶ αὐτοῦ. 31 καὶ ἤρξατο διδάσκειν
them, that no one they may tell about Him. And He began to teach

30 And he charged them that they should tell no man of him.

31. And He began to teach them that it is necessary for the Son of man to suffer many things, and to be rejected of the elders and chief priests and scribes, and to be killed, and after three days to rise again.

846 3754 1163 3588 5207 3588 444 4183 3958 2532
αὐτοὺς, ὅτι δεῖ τὸν υἱὸν τοῦ ἀνθρώπου πολλὰ παθεῖν, καὶ
them, that must the Son of man many things to suffer, and

593 575 3588 4245 2532 749 2532
ἀποδοκιμασθῆναι ἀπὸ τῶν πρεσβυτέρων καὶ ἀρχιερέων καὶ
to be rejected from the elders and chief priests and

1122 2532 615 2532 3326 5140 2250
γραμματέων, καὶ ἀποκτανθῆναι, καὶ μετὰ τρεῖς ἡμέρας
scribes, and to be killed, and after three days

31. And he began to teach them, that the Son of man must suffer many things, and be rejected of the elders, and (of) the chief priests, and scribes, and be killed, and after three days rise again.

450 2532 3954 3588 3056 2980 2532 4355
ἀναστῆναι· 32 καὶ παρρησίᾳ τὸν λόγον ἐλάλει. καὶ προσλαβό-
to rise again. And openly the word He spoke. And having taken

32 And He spoke the word openly. And taking Him aside, Peter began to rebuke Him.

846 3588 4074 756 2008 846 3588 1161 1994
μενος αὐτὸν ὁ Πέτρος ἤρξατο ἐπιτιμᾶν αὐτῷ. 33 ὁ δὲ ἐπιστρα-
aside Him Peter began to rebuke Him. He But turning

32 And he spake that saying openly. And Peter took him, and began to rebuke him.

33 But turning around and seeing His disciples, He rebuked Peter, saying, Go behind Me, Satan, because you do not mind the things of God, but the things of men.

2532 1492 3588 3101 846 2008 3588 4074
φεὶς, καὶ ἰδὼν τοὺς μαθητὰς αὐτοῦ, ἐπετίμησε τῷ Πέτρῳ,
around and seeing the disciples of Him rebuked Peter,

3004 5217 3694 3450 4567 3754 3756 5426 3588 3588 3588
λέγων, Ὕπαγε ὀπίσω μου, Σατανᾶ, ὅτι οὐ φρονεῖς τὰ τοῦ
saying, Go behind Me, Satan, because not you mind the things

2316 235 3588 3588 444 2532 4341 3588
Θεοῦ, ἀλλὰ τὰ τῶν ἀνθρώπων. 34 καὶ προσκαλεσάμενος τὸν
of God, but the things of men. And having called near the

33 But when he had turned about and looked on his disciples, he rebuked Peter, saying, Get thee behind me, Satan: for thou savourest not the things that be of God, but the things that be of men.

34. And having called near the crowd with His disciples, He said to them, Whoever desires to come after Me, let him deny himself and take his cross, and let him follow Me.

3793 4862 3588 3101 846 2036 846 3748 2309
ὄχλον σὺν τοῖς μαθηταῖς αὐτοῦ, εἶπεν αὐτοῖς, Ὅστις θέλει
crowd with the disciples of Him, He said to them, Whoever desires

3694 3450 2064 533 1438 2532 142 3588
ὀπίσω μου ἐλθεῖν, ἀπαρνησάσθω ἑαυτὸν, καὶ ἀράτω τὸν
after Me to come, let him deny himself, and take the

34. And when he had called the people (unto him) with his disciples also, he said unto them, Whosoever will come after me, let him deny himself, and take up his cross, and follow me.

4716 846 2532 190 3427 3739 1063 302 2309 3588
σταυρὸν αὐτοῦ, καὶ ἀκολουθείτω μοι. 35 ὃς γὰρ ἂν θέλῃ τὴν
cross of him, and let him follow Me. who For ever desires the

35 For whoever desires to save his life, (he) shall lose it. But whoever shall lose his life for My sake and the gospel, that one shall save it.

5590 846 4982 622 846 3739 1161 302 622 3588
ψυχὴν αὐτοῦ σῶσαι, ἀπολέσει αὐτήν· ὃς δ' ἂν ἀπολέσῃ τὴν
life of him to save, shall lose it. who But ever may lose the

5590 846 1752 1700 2532 3588 2098 3778 4982
ψυχὴν αὐτοῦ ἕνεκεν ἐμοῦ καὶ τοῦ εὐαγγελίου, οὗτος σώσει
life of him for the sake of Me and the gospel, this one will save

35 For whosoever will save his life shall lose it; but whosoever shall lose his life for my sake and the gospel's, the same shall save it.

36 For what shall it profit a man if he gain the whole world, yet forfeit his soul?

846 5101 1063 5623 444 1437 2770 3588
αὐτήν. 36 τί γὰρ ὠφελήσει ἄνθρωπον, ἐὰν κερδήσῃ τὸν
it. what For shall it profit a man, if he gain the

2889 3650 2532 2210 3588 5590 846 2228 5101 4982
κόσμον ὅλον, καὶ ζημιωθῇ τὴν ψυχὴν αὐτοῦ; 37 ἢ τί δώσει
world whole, yet forfeit the soul of him? Or what shall give

36 For what shall it profit a man, if he shall gain the whole world, and lose his own soul?

37 Or what shall a man give

37 Or what shall a man give

Literal Translation

(as) an exchange (for) his soul?
38 For whoever may be ashamed of Me and My words in this adulterous and sinful generation, the Son of man will also be ashamed of him when He comes in the glory of His Father, along with the holy angels.

Mark 8:38

444 465 3588 5590 846 3739 1063 302 1870
ἄνθρωπος ἀντάλλαγμα τῆς ψυχῆς αὐτοῦ; 38 ὃς γὰρ ἂν ἐπαι-
a man (as) an exchange (for) the soul of him? who For ever may be

3165 2532 3588 1699 3056 1722 3588 1074 3778 3588
σχυνθῇ με καὶ τοὺς ἐμοὺς λόγους ἐν τῇ γενεᾷ ταύτῃ τῇ
ashamed of Me and My words in generation this

3428 2532 268 2532 3588 5207 3588 444 1870
μοιχαλίδι καὶ ἁμαρτωλῷ, καὶ ὁ υἱὸς τοῦ ἀνθρώπου ἐπαι-
adulterous and sinful, also the Son of man will

846 3752 2064 1722 3588 1391 3588 3962
σχυνθήσεται αὐτὸν, ὅταν ἔλθῃ ἐν τῇ δόξῃ τοῦ πατρὸς
be ashamed of him, when He comes in the glory of the Father

846 3326 3588 32 3588 40
αὐτοῦ μετὰ τῶν ἀγγέλων τῶν ἁγίων.
of Him with the angels holy.

King James Version

in exchange for his soul?
38 Whosoever therefore shall be ashamed of me and of my words in this adulterous and sinful generation; of him also shall the Son of man be ashamed, when he cometh in the glory of his Father with the holy angels.

The following is the full chapter, in English and in Greek of Mark: Chapter 13, Verse 32, where acrostic 4 begins, is clearly marked.

1. And He having gone out of the temple, one of His disciples said to Him, Teacher, Behold! What kind of stones and what kind of buildings!

```
   2552         1607          846  1537 3588 2411   3004    846  1520
1. Καὶ ἐκπορευομένου αὐτοῦ ἐκ τοῦ ἱεροῦ, λέγει αὐτῷ εἷς
   And    having gone forth   He out of the temple,  says  to Him  one
   3588      3101        846      1320     2396    4217     3037   2532
   τῶν   μαθητῶν αὐτοῦ, Διδάσκαλε, ἴδε, ποταποὶ λίθοι καὶ
   of the  disciples   of Him,   Teacher,   behold.  what kind of stones and
   4217        3619          2532 3588 2424    611         2036   846
   ποταποὶ οἰκοδομαί. 2 καὶ ὁ Ἰησοῦς ἀποκριθεὶς εἶπεν αὐτῷ,
   what kind of buildings!   And  Jesus    answering    said   to him,
```

1. And as he went out of the temple, one of his disciples saith unto him, Master, see what manner of stones and what buildings (are here)!

2 And answering, Jesus said to him, Do you see these great buildings? Not at all one stone shall be left upon a stone which shall not be demolished, none.

```
   991      3778    3588   3173      3619     3756 3361 863   3037
   Βλέπεις ταύτας τὰς μεγάλας οἰκοδομάς; οὐ μὴ ἀφεθῇ λίθος
   Do you see these        great      buildings?  Not at all will be left stone
   1909 3037 3739 3756 3361 2647
   ἐπὶ λίθῳ ὃς οὐ μὴ καταλυθῇ.
   on  stone which not at all (will) be demolished.
```

2 And Jesus answering said unto him, Seest thou these great buildings? there shall not be left one stone upon another, that shall not be thrown down.

3 And (as) He (was) sitting in the Mount of Olives opposite the temple, Peter and James and John and Andrew questioned Him privately:

```
    2532      2521          846   1519 3588 3735 3588  1636     2713
3. Καὶ καθημένου αὐτοῦ εἰς τὸ ὄρος τῶν ἐλαιῶν κατέναντι
   And    sitting       He   in  the  Mount of the Olives    opposite
   3588 2411       1905       846    2596  2398     4074    2532  2385
   τοῦ ἱεροῦ, ἐπηρώτων αὐτὸν κατ' ἰδίαν Πέτρος καὶ Ἰάκωβος
   the  temple,   questioned  Him  privately        Peter   and   James
   2532   2491        2532    406       2036   2254  4219   5023   2071
   καὶ Ἰωάννης καὶ Ἀνδρέας, 4 Εἰπὲ ἡμίν, πότε ταῦτα ἔσται;
   and    John   and  Andrew,   Tell us, when these things will be?
```

3 And as he sat upon the mount of Olives over against the temple, Peter and James and John and Andrew asked him privately,

4 Tell us when these things shall be? And what (is) the sign when all these things are about to be completed?

```
   2532 5101 3588  4592      3752   3195    3956   5023        4931
   καὶ τί τὸ σημεῖον ὅταν μέλλη πάντα ταῦτα συντελεῖσθαι;
   And what (is) the sign  when are about  all   these things to be completed?
```

4 Tell us, when shall these things be? and what (shall be) the sign when all these things shall be fulfilled?

5 And answering, Jesus began to say to them, Look out that no one lead you astray.

```
   3588 1161 2424       611        846     756     3004    991   3361 5100
5 ὁ δὲ Ἰησοῦς ἀποκριθεὶς αὐτοῖς ἤρξατο λέγειν, Βλέπετε μή τις
   And Jesus    answering     to them  began  to say,  Beware  not anyone
   5209    4105        4183   1063   2064      1909 3588 3686   3450
   ὑμᾶς πλανήσῃ. 6 πολλοὶ γὰρ ἐλεύσονται ἐπὶ τῷ ὀνόματί μου,
   you  lead astray      many    For   will come    on  the  name  of Me,
```

5 And Jesus answering them began to say, Take heed lest any (man) deceive you:

6 For many will come on My name, saying, I AM! And they will lead many astray.
7 But when

```
   3004      3754 1473 1510 2532 4183         4105      3752 1161
   λέγοντες ὅτι Ἐγώ εἰμι· καὶ πολλοὺς πλανήσουσιν. 7 ὅταν δὲ
   saying.       I  AM!   And  many   they will lead astray. when But
```

6 For many shall come in my name, saying, I am (Christ); and shall deceive many.
7 And when

Literal Translation

you hear (of) wars and rumors of wars, do not be alarmed, for it must occur, but the end (is) not yet.
8 For nation will be aroused against nation, and kingdom against kingdom. And there shall be earthquakes (in) various places. And there shall be famines and agitations. These things (are) the beginnings of travails.

9. But you yourselves look out, for they will deliver you up to sanhedrins and to synagogues. You will be flogged, and you will be led before rulers and kings for My sake, for a testimony to them.

10 And the gospel must first be proclaimed to all the nations.
11 But whenever they lead (you) away, delivering (you), do not be anxious beforehand, what you should say, nor meditate. But whatever may be given to you in that hour, speak that. For you are not those speaking, but the Holy Spirit.
12 And a brother will deliver up a brother to death, and a father a child. And children will rise up on parents and will put them to death.
13 And you will be hated by all on account of My name. But the (one) enduring to the end, this (one) will be kept safe.

14. But when you see the abomination of desolation, the (one) spoken of by Daniel the prophet, standing where it ought not (the reading, let him understand), then let those in Judea flee into the mountains. (Dan. 11:31; 12:11)
15. And he on the housetop, let him not go down into the house.

Greek Interlinear

191   4171   2532   189   4171   3361   2360   1163
ἀκούσητε πολέμους καὶ ἀκοὰς πολέμων, μὴ θροεῖσθε· δεῖ
you hear (o:) wars and rumors of wars, not be alarmed. it must

1063   1096   235   3768 3588 5056   1453   1063 1484
γὰρ γενέσθαι· ἀλλ᾽ οὔπω τὸ τέλος. 8 ἐγερθήσεται γὰρ ἔθνος
for occur. but not yet the end. will be aroused For nation

1909 1484   2532   932   1909   932   2532   2071   4578
ἐπὶ ἔθνος, καὶ βασιλεία ἐπὶ βασιλείαν· καὶ ἔσονται σεισμοὶ
against nation, and kingdom against kingdom. And shall be earthquakes

2596   5117   2532   2071   3042 2532 5016   746   5604
κατὰ τόπους, καὶ ἔσονται λιμοὶ καὶ ταραχαί· ἀρχαὶ ὠδίνων
(in) various places, and shall be famines and agitations; beginnings of travails

5023
ταῦτα.
These things (are).

991   1161 5210   1438   3860   1063 5209 1519
9. βλέπετε δὲ ὑμεῖς ἑαυτούς· παραδώσουσι γὰρ ὑμᾶς εἰς
look out But you yourselves; they will deliver up for you to

4892   2532 1519   4864   1194   2532 1909   2232
συνέδρια, καὶ εἰς συναγωγὰς δαρήσεσθε, καὶ ἐπὶ ἡγεμόνων
sanhedrins, and to synagogues you will be flogged, and before rulers

2532   935   2476   1752   1700 1519   3142   846
καὶ βασιλέων ἀχθήσεσθε ἕνεκεν ἐμοῦ, εἰς μαρτύριον αὐτοῖς·
and kings you will be led for the sake of Me, for a testimony to them.

2532 1519 3956 3588 1484 1163 4412   2784   3588   2098
10 καὶ εἰς πάντα τὰ ἔθνη δεῖ πρῶτον κηρυχθῆναι τὸ εὐαγγέλιον.
And to all the nations must first be proclaimed the gospel.

3752 1161   71   5209   3860   3361   4305   5101
11 ὅταν δὲ ἀγάγωσιν ὑμᾶς παραδιδόντες, μὴ προμεριμνᾶτε τί
when And they lead away you, delivering (you), not be anxious before what

2980   3366   3191   235 3739 1437 1325   5213 1722 1565 3588
λαλήσητε, μηδὲ μελετᾶτε· ἀλλ᾽ ὃ ἐὰν δοθῇ ὑμῖν ἐν ἐκείνῃ τῇ
you shall say, nor meditate; but whatever is given to you in that

5610   5124   2980   3756 1063 2075 5210 3588   2980   235
ὥρᾳ, τοῦτο λαλεῖτε· οὐ γάρ ἐστε ὑμεῖς οἱ λαλοῦντες, ἀλλὰ
hour, this speak; not for are you the (one) speaking, but

3588 4151 3588   40   3860   1161   80   80   1519
τὸ Πνεῦμα τὸ Ἅγιον. 12 παραδώσει δὲ ἀδελφὸς ἀδελφὸν εἰς
the Spirit Holy. will deliver up But a brother a brother to

2288   2532 3962   5043   2532   1881   5043 1909
θάνατον, καὶ πατὴρ τέκνον· καὶ ἐπαναστήσονται τέκνα ἐπὶ
death, and a father a child, and will rise up children upon

1118   2532   2289   846   2532   2071   3404
γονεῖς, καὶ θανατώσουσιν αὐτούς· 13 καὶ ἔσεσθε μισούμενοι
parents, and put to death them. And you will be hated

5259   3956   1223 3588   3686   3450 3588 1161   5278   1519 5056
ὑπὸ πάντων διὰ τὸ ὄνομά μου· ὁ δὲ ὑπομείνας εἰς τέλος,
by all on account of the name of Me he But enduring to the end,

3778   4982
οὗτος σωθήσεται.
this (one) will be kept safe

3752   1161 1492 3588   946   3588   2050   3588   4483
14. Ὅταν δὲ ἴδητε τὸ βδέλυγμα τῆς ἐρημώσεως, τὸ ῥηθὲν
when But you see the abomination of desolation, that spoken

5259   1158   3588   4396   2476   3699 3756 1163 3588   314
ὑπὸ Δανιὴλ τοῦ προφήτου, ἑστὼς ὅπου οὐ δεῖ ὁ ἀναγινώ-
by Daniel the prophet, standing where not it ought (he reading,

3539   5119 3588 1722 3588   2449   5343   1519 3588
σκων νοείτω), τότε οἱ ἐν τῇ Ἰουδαίᾳ φευγέτωσαν εἰς τὰ
let him understand), then those in Judea let them flee into the

3735   3588 1161 1909 3588   1430   3361 2597   1519 3588   3614
ὄρη· 15 ὁ δὲ ἐπὶ τοῦ δώματος μὴ καταβάτω εἰς τὴν οἰκίαν,
mounts, he and on the housetop not let him descend into the house,

King James Version

ye shall hear of wars and rumours of wars, be ye not troubled: for (such things) must needs be; but the end (shall) not (be) yet.
8 For nation shall rise against nation, and kingdom against kingdom: and there shall be earthquakes in divers places, and there shall be famines and troubles: these (are) the beginnings of sorrows.

9. But take heed to yourselves: for they shall deliver you up to councils; and in the synagogues ye shall be beaten: and ye shall be brought before rulers and kings for my sake, for a testimony against them.

10 And the gospel must first be published among all nations.
11 But when they shall lead (you), and deliver you up, take no thought beforehand what ye shall speak, neither do ye premeditate: but whatsoever shall be given you in that hour, that speak ye: for it is not ye that speak, but the Holy Ghost.
12 Now the brother shall betray the brother to death, and the father the son; and children shall rise up against (their) parents, and shall cause them to be put to death.
13 And ye shall be hated of all (men) for my name's sake: but he that shall endure unto the end, the same shall be saved.

14. But when ye shall see the abomination of desolation, spoken of by Daniel the prophet, standing where it ought not, (let him that readeth understand,) then let them that be in Judea flee to the mountains:
15 And let him that is on the housetop not go down into the house,

Literal Translation

nor go in to take a thing out of his house.
16 And the one in the field, let him not return to the things behind to take his garment.

17 But woe to those holding (a babe) in womb, and to those giving suck in those days!
18 And pray that your flight may not occur in winter.
19 for there will be affliction (in) those days, such as has not been the like from (the) beginning of creation which God created until now, and not at all may be.
20 And if (the) Lord had not shortened the days, not any flesh would be saved; but because of the elect whom He elected, He shortened the days.
21 And then if anyone says to you, Behold, here (is) the Christ! Or, Behold, there! Do not believe.

22 For false christs and false prophets will be raised, and they will give signs and wonders in order to lead astray, if possible, even the elect.

23 But you be careful. Behold, I have foretold you all things.

24. But in those days, after that affliction, the sun will be darkened, and the moon will not give her light;

25 and the stars of the heaven will be falling, and the powers in the heavens will be shaken.
26 And then they will see the Son of man coming in clouds with much power and glory. (Dan 7:13)

27 And then He will send His angels and will gather His elect from

Interlinear

3366   1525   142 5100 1537 3588 3614   846   2532 3588 1519 3588
μηδὲ εἰσελθέτω ἆραί τι ἐκ τῆς οἰκίας αὐτοῦ· 16 καὶ ὁ εἰς τὸν
nor let him enter to take a thing out of the house of him.   And the (one) in the

68   5607 3361   1994   1519 3588 3694   142 3588   2440
ἀγρὸν ὢν μὴ ἐπιστρεψάτω εἰς τὰ ὀπίσω, ἆραι τὸ ἱμάτιον
field being, not let him go back to the things behind, to take the garment

846   3759 1161 3588 1722 1064   2192   2532 3588   2337
αὐτοῦ. 17 οὐαὶ δὲ ταῖς ἐν γαστρὶ ἐχούσαις καὶ ταῖς θηλαζού-
of him.   woe But to those in womb holding, and to those giving

1722 1565   3588   2250   4336   1161 2443 3361 1096
σαις ἐν ἐκείναις ταῖς ἡμέραις. 18 προσεύχεσθε δὲ ἵνα μὴ γένηται
suck in those   days   pray   But that not may occur

3588 5437 5216   5494   2071   1063 3588 2250   1565   2347
ἡ φυγὴ ὑμῶν χειμῶνος. 19 ἔσονται γὰρ αἱ ἡμέραι ἐκεῖναι θλίψις,
the flight of you in winter.   will be For   days those affliction

3634 3756 1096   5108   575   746   2937   3739   2936 3588
οἷα οὐ γέγονε τοιαύτη ἀπ᾽ ἀρχῆς κτίσεως ἧς ἔκτισεν ὁ
such as not has been the like from beginning of creation which created

2316 2193 3588 3568 2532 3756 3361   1096   2532 1487 3361 2962
Θεὸς ἕως τοῦ νῦν, καὶ οὐ μὴ γένηται. 20 καὶ εἰ μὴ Κύριος
God until now, and not at all may be.   And except (the) Lord

2856   3588   2250   3756 302 4982   3956 4561   235 1223
ἐκολόβωσε τὰς ἡμέρας, οὐκ ἂν ἐσώθη πᾶσα σάρξ· ἀλλὰ διὰ
had shortened the days, not would be saved any flesh; but because of

3588   1588   3739 1586   2856   3588 2250   2532
τοὺς ἐκλεκτούς, οὓς ἐξελέξατο, ἐκολόβωσε τὰς ἡμέρας. 21 καὶ
the elect, whom He elected, He shortened the days   And

5119 1437 5100 5213 2036 2400 5602 3588 5547   2228 2400 1563 3361
τότε ἐάν τις ὑμῖν εἴπῃ, Ἰδού, ὧδε ὁ Χριστός, ἢ Ἰδού, ἐκεῖ, μὴ
then if anyone to you says, Behold! Here (is) the Christ, or, behold, there, not

4100   1453   1063   5580   2532   5578
πιστεύσητε. 22 ἐγερθήσονται γὰρ ψευδόχριστοι καὶ ψευδο-
do believe   will be raised For false christs and false

2532   1325   4592   2532 5059   4314 3588 635
προφῆται, καὶ δώσουσι σημεῖα καὶ τέρατα, πρὸς τὸ ἀπο-
prophets. and they will give signs and wonders in order to lead

1487 1415   2532 3588   1588   5210 1161 991
πλανᾶν, εἰ δυνατόν, καὶ τοὺς ἐκλεκτούς. 23 ὑμεῖς δὲ βλέπετε·
astray, if it could be, even the elect.   you But look out

2400   4280   5213 3956
ἰδού, προείρηκα ὑμῖν πάντα.
Behold! I have told before you all things.

235 1722 1565   3588   2250   3326 3588 2347   1565
24. Ἀλλ᾽ ἐν ἐκείναις ταῖς ἡμέραις, μετὰ τὴν θλίψιν ἐκείνην,
But in those   days, after the affliction that,

3588 2246   4654   2532 3588 4582 3756 1325 3588 5338
ὁ ἥλιος σκοτισθήσεται, καὶ ἡ σελήνη οὐ δώσει τὸ φέγγος
the sun will be darkened, and the moon not will give the light

846   2532 3588 792   3588   3772   2071   1601
αὐτῆς, 25 καὶ οἱ ἀστέρες τοῦ οὐρανοῦ ἔσονται ἐκπίπτοντες,
of her, and the stars of the heaven will be falling,

2532 3588 1411   3588 1722 3588 3772   4531   2532 5119
καὶ αἱ δυνάμεις αἱ ἐν τοῖς οὐρανοῖς σαλευθήσονται. 26 καὶ τότε
and the powers in the heavens will be shaken. And then

3700   3588 5207 3588   444   2064   1722   3507
ὄψονται τὸν υἱὸν τοῦ ἀνθρώπου ἐρχόμενον ἐν νεφέλαις
they will see the Son of man coming in clouds

3326 1411   4183 2532 1391   2532 5119   649   3588
μετὰ δυνάμεως πολλῆς καὶ δόξης. 27 καὶ τότε ἀποστελεῖ τοὺς
with power much and glory.   And then He will send the

32   846 2532   1996   3588   1588   846 1537
ἀγγέλους αὐτοῦ, καὶ ἐπισυνάξει τοὺς ἐκλεκτοὺς αὐτοῦ ἐκ
angels of Him, and they will gather the elect of Him out of

King James Version

neither enter (therein), to take any thing out of his house:
16 And let him that is in the field not turn back again for to take up his garment.

17 But woe to them that are with child, and to them that give suck in those days!
18 And pray ye that your flight be not in the winter.
19 For (in) those days shall be affliction, such as was not from the beginning of the creation which God created unto this time, neither shall be.
20 And except that the Lord had shortened those days, no flesh should be saved: but for the elect's sake, whom he hath chosen, he hath shortened the days.
21 And then if any man shall say to you, Lo, here (is) Christ; or, lo, (he is) there; believe (him) not:

22 For false Christs and false prophets shall rise, and shall shew signs and wonders, to seduce, if (it were) possible, even the elect.

23 But take ye heed: behold, I have foretold you all things.

24. But in those days, after that tribulation, the sun shall be darkened, and the moon shall not give her light,

25 And the stars of heaven shall fall, and the powers that are in heaven shall be shaken.
26 And then shall they see the Son of man coming in the clouds with great power and glory.

27 And then shall he send his angels, and shall gather together his elect from

the four winds, from (the) end of earth to (the) end of (the) heaven.

3588	5064	417	575	206	1093	2193	206	3772
τῶν	τεσσάρων	ἀνέμων,	ἀπ'	ἄκρου	γῆς	ἕως	ἄκρου	οὐρανοῦ.
the	four	winds,	from (the) end of earth until (the) end of (the) heaven.					

the four winds, from the uttermost part of the earth to the uttermost part of heaven.

28 And from the fig tree learn the parable: When its branch becomes tender and puts out leaves, you know the summer is near.

575	1161	3588	4808	3129	3588	3850	3752	846
28 Ἀπὸ	δὲ	τῆς	συκῆς	μάθετε	τὴν	παραβολήν·	ὅταν	αὐτῆς
from	And	the	fig-tree	learn	the	parable:	when	of it

2235	3588	2798	527	1096	2532	1631	3588	5444	1097
ἤδη	ὁ	κλάδος	ἀπαλὸς	γένηται	καὶ	ἐκφύῃ	τὰ	φύλλα,	γινώ-
now	the	branch	tender	becomes	and	puts out	the	leaves,	you

28 Now learn a parable of the fig tree; When her branch is yet tender, and putteth forth leaves, ye know that summer is near:

29 So you also, when you see these things happening, know that it is near, at (the) doors.

3754	1451	3588	2330	2076	3779	2532	5210	3752	5023
σκετε	ὅτι	ἐγγὺς	τὸ	θέρος	ἐστίν·	29 οὕτω	καὶ	ὑμεῖς,	ὅταν	ταῦτα
know that	near	the	summer	is.	So also you,	when these things			

1492	1096	1097	3754	1451	2076	1909	2374	281
ἴδητε	γινόμενα,	γινώσκετε	ὅτι	ἐγγύς	ἐστιν	ἐπὶ	θύραις.	30 ἀμὴν
you see happening,	know	that	near	it is,	at (the) doors.			Truly

29 So ye in like manner, when ye shall see these things come to pass, know that it is nigh, (even) at the doors.

30 Truly I say to you, Not at all will this generation pass away until all these things occur.

3004	5213	3754	3756	3361	3928	3588	1074	846	3360	3756
λέγω	ὑμῖν	ὅτι	οὐ	μὴ	παρέλθῃ	ἡ	γενεὰ	αὕτη,	μέχρις	οὗ
I say to you	that	in no way	will pass away	generation	this	until	not			

3956	5023	1096	3588	3772	2532	3588	1093	3928
πάντα	ταῦτα	γένηται.	31 ὁ	οὐρανὸς	καὶ	ἡ	γῆ	παρελεύσονται·
all	these things occur.		The heaven	and	the earth will pass away;			

30 Verily I say unto you, that this generation shall not pass, till all these things be done.

31 The heaven and the earth will pass away, but My words will not pass away, never!

3588	1161	3056	3450	3756	3361	3928	4012	1161	3588	2250
οἱ	δὲ	λόγοι	μου	οὐ	μὴ	παρέλθωσι.	32 περὶ	δὲ	τῆς	ἡμέρας
the	but	words	of Me	not	never will pass away.		concerning	But		day

31 Heaven and earth shall pass away: but my words shall not pass away.

32. But concerning that day and the hour, no one knows, not the angels, those in Heaven, not the Son, except the Father.

1565	2532	3588	5610	3762	1492	3761	3588	32	3588	1722
ἐκείνης	καὶ	τῆς	ὥρας	οὐδεὶς	οἶδεν,	οὐδὲ	οἱ	ἄγγελοι	οἱ	ἐν
that	and	the	hour	no one	knows,	not	the	angels	those in

3772	3761	3588	5207	1487	3361	3588	3962	991	69
οὐρανῷ,	οὐδὲ	ὁ	υἱός,	εἰ	μὴ	ὁ	πατήρ.	33 βλέπετε,	ἀγρυπνεῖτε
Heaven,	nor	the Son,	except	the Father.		Look out!,	Be wakeful		

32. But of that day and (that) hour knoweth no man, no, not the angels which are in heaven, neither the Son, but the Father.

33 Watch! Be wakeful, and pray! For you do not know when the time is.

2532	4336	3756	1492	1063	4219	3588	2540	2076	5613
καὶ	προσεύχεσθε·	οὐκ	οἴδατε	γὰρ	πότε	ὁ	καιρός	ἐστιν.	34 ὡς
and	pray!	not	you know	For	when	the	time	is.	As

33 Take ye heed, watch and pray: for ye know not when the time is.

34 As a man going away, leaving his house, and giving his slaves authority, and to each his work (and he commanded the door-keeper, that he should watch),

444	590	863	3588	3614	846	2532	1325	3588
ἄνθρωπος	ἀπόδημος	ἀφεὶς	τὴν	οἰκίαν	αὐτοῦ,	καὶ	δοὺς	τοῖς
a man	going away	leaving	the	house	of him,	and	giving to the	

1401	846	3588	1849	2532	1538	3588	2041	846
δούλοις	αὐτοῦ	τὴν	ἐξουσίαν,	καὶ	ἑκάστῳ	τὸ	ἔργον	αὐτοῦ,
slaves	of him	the	authority,	and	to each	the	work	of him,

34 (For the Son of man is) as a man taking a far journey, who left his house, and gave authority to his servants, and to every man his work, and commanded the porter to watch.

2532	3588	2377	1781	2443	1127	1127	3767
καὶ	τῷ	θυρωρῷ	ἐνετείλατο	ἵνα	γρηγορῇ.	35 γρηγορεῖτε	οὖν·
and	the	doorkeeper	he ordered	that	he should watch.	You watch	then;

35 then you watch, for you do not know when the lord of the house is coming, evening, or midnight, or at cock-crowing, or at dawn;

3756	1492	1063	4219	3588	2962	3588	3614	2064	3796	2228
οὐκ	οἴδατε	γὰρ	πότε	ὁ	κύριος	τῆς	οἰκίας	ἔρχεται,	ὀψέ,	ἢ
not	you know	For	when	the lord	of the house			comes,	evening or	

35 Watch ye therefore: for ye know not when the master of the house cometh, at even, or at midnight, or at the cock-crowing, or in the morning:

3317	2228	219	2228	4404	3361	2064	1810
μεσονυκτίου,	ἢ	ἀλεκτοροφωνίας,	ἢ	πρωΐ·	36 μὴ	ἐλθὼν	ἐξαίφνης
midnight,	or	at cock-crowing,	or	at dawn,	(that) not	coming	suddenly

36 so that not coming suddenly he find you sleeping.

2147	5209	2518	3739	1161	5213	3004	3956	3004
εὕρῃ	ὑμᾶς	καθεύδοντας.	37 ἃ	δὲ	ὑμῖν	λέγω	πᾶσι	λέγω,
he find	you	sleeping.	what	And	to you	I say,	to all	I say,

36 Lest coming suddenly he find you sleeping.

37 And what I say to you, I say to all. Watch!

| 1127 |
| Γρηγορεῖτε. |
| Watch! |

37 And what I say unto you I say unto all, Watch.

Acrostic Index

The following is the full chapter, in English and in Greek of Luke: Chapter 9, Verse 23, where acrostic 5 begins, is clearly marked.

1. And having called together His twelve disciples, He gave them power and authority over all the demons, and to heal diseases.

2 And (He) sent them to proclaim the kingdom of God, and to heal the ones being sick.
3 And He said to them, Take nothing for the way, neither staffs, nor money bag, nor bread, nor silver, nor each to have two tunics.

4 And into whatever house you enter, remain there, and go out from there.
5 And as many as may not receive you, going out from that city even shake off the dust from your feet, for a testimony against them.

6 And going out, they passed through the villages, preaching the gospel, and healing everywhere.


```
            4779              1161 3588    1427      3101         846    1325
  1  Συγκαλεσάμενος  δὲ  τοὺς  δώδεκα  μαθητὰς  αὐτοῦ,  ἔδωκεν
     having called together And the     twelve  disciples  of Him,  He gave
       846      1411    2532   1849     1909  3956  3588   1140    2532
     αὐτοῖς  δύναμιν  καὶ  ἐξουσίαν  ἐπὶ  πάντα  τὰ  δαιμόνια,  καὶ
     to them  power    and  authority  over  all   the  demons,    and
     3554         2323       2532   649        846        2784     3588
     νόσους  θεραπεύειν,  2 καὶ  ἀπέστειλεν  αὐτοὺς  κηρύσσειν  τὴν
     diseases  to heal.      And  He sent      them    to proclaim  the
       932      3588 2316  2532  2390  3588    770         2532 2036
     βασιλείαν  τοῦ Θεοῦ,  καὶ  ἰᾶσθαι  τοὺς  ἀσθενοῦντας.  3 καὶ  εἶπε
     kingdom    of God, and to heal  those  being sick.     And He said
     4314  846     3367    142    1519 3588  3598   3383     4464
     πρὸς  αὐτούς,  Μηδὲν  αἴρετε  εἰς  τὴν  ὁδόν·  μήτε  ῥάβδους,
     to    them,   Nothing  take   for  the  way,   neither  staffs,
     3383    4082     3383   740    3383    694      3383   303   1417
     μήτε  πήραν,   μήτε  ἄρτον,  μήτε  ἀργύριον,  μήτε  ἀνὰ  δύο
     nor   money bag,  nor   bread,  nor   silver,    nor   each  two
     5509      2192    2532 1519 3739 302 3614        1525      1563 3306
     χιτῶνας  ἔχειν.  4 καὶ  εἰς  ἣν  ἂν  οἰκίαν  εἰσέλθητε,  ἐκεῖ  μένετε,
     tunics    to have.  And into whatever house  you enter,   there  remain.
     2532  1564    1831              2532  3745 302 3361  1209      5209
     καὶ  ἐκεῖθεν  ἐξέρχεσθε.  5 καὶ  ὅσοι  ἂν  μὴ  δέξωνται  ὑμᾶς,
     and  from there  go out.        And  as many as  not  may receive  you,
        1831       575 3588   4172    1565   2532 3588   2868     575
     ἐξερχόμενοι  ἀπὸ  τῆς  πόλεως  ἐκείνης  καὶ  τὸν  κονιορτὸν  ἀπὸ
     going out   from       city     that    even  the   dust      from
     3588   4228    5216    660     1519   3142     1909    846
     τῶν  ποδῶν  ὑμῶν  ἀποτινάξατε  εἰς  μαρτύριον  ἐπ'  αὐτούς.
     the   feet   of you  shake off,   for  a testimony  against  them.
        1831      1161   1330     2596 3588 2968          2097
     6 ἐξερχόμενοι  δὲ  διήρχοντο  κατὰ  τὰς  κώμας,  εὐαγγελιζόμενοι
     going out    And  they passed  through the villages  preaching the gospel
     2532    2323          3837
     καὶ  θεραπεύοντες  πανταχοῦ.
     and   healing        everywhere.
```


1. Then he called his twelve disciples together, and gave them power and authority over all devils, and to cure diseases.

2 And he sent them to preach the kingdom of God, and to heal the sick.

3 And he said unto them, Take nothing for (your) journey, neither staves, nor scrip, neither bread, neither money; neither have two coats apiece.

4 And whatsoever house ye enter into, there abide, and thence depart.

5 And whosoever will not receive you, when ye go out of that city, shake off the very dust from your feet for a testimony against them.

6 And they departed, and went through the towns, preaching the gospel, and healing every where.

Literal Translation (left column):

7. And Herod the tetrarch heard all the things happening by Him, and was perplexed, because of the saying by some that John had been raised from (the) dead, 8 and by some that Elijah had appeared. And others that a prophet of the ancients rose again.

9 And Herod said, I beheaded John, but who is this about whom I hear such things? And he sought to see Him.

10. And having returned, the apostles told Him what things they did. And taking them He withdrew privately to a deserted place of a city being called Bethsaida. 11 But knowing (this), the crowds followed Him. And having received them, He spoke to them about the kingdom of God. And He cured those having need of healing.

12. But the day began to decline. And coming up the Twelve said to Him, Let the crowd go that going to the surrounding villages and the farms they may lodge and find food supplies, because here we are in a deserted place.

13 But He said to them, You give them to eat. But they said, There are not to us more than five loaves and two fish, unless going we buy foods for all this people.

14 For there were about five thousand men. But He said to His disciples, cause them to recline

Greek interlinear (center column):

7. ῾Ηκουσε δὲ ῾Ηρῴδης ὁ τετράρχης τὰ γινόμενα ὑπ' αὐτοῦ
    hearing And   Herod   the tetrarch   the things happening by   Him

πάντα· καὶ διηπόρει διὰ τὸ λέγεσθαι ὑπό τινων ὅτι
all,   and was perplexed, because of the   saying   by   some   that

Ἰωάννης ἐγήγερται ἐκ νεκρῶν· 8 ὑπό τινων δὲ ὅτι ῾Ηλίας
John   has been raised from (the) dead,   by   some   and that   Elijah

ἐφάνη· ἄλλων δὲ ὅτι Προφήτης εἷς τῶν ἀρχαίων ἀνέστη·
had appeared, others and that   a prophet   of the   ancients   rose again.

9 καὶ εἶπεν ὁ ῾Ηρῴδης, Ἰωάννην ἐγὼ ἀπεκεφάλισα· τίς δέ
And   said   Herod.   John   I   beheaded,   who but

ἐστιν οὗτος, περὶ οὗ ἐγὼ ἀκούω τοιαῦτα; καὶ ἐζήτει ἰδεῖν
is   this   about whom I   hear   such things? And   he sought to see

αὐτόν.
Him.

10. Καὶ ὑποστρέψαντες οἱ ἀπόστολοι διηγήσαντο αὐτῷ ὅσα
    And having returned   the   apostles   told   Him   what things

ἐποίησαν. καὶ παραλαβὼν αὐτούς, ὑπεχώρησε κατ' ἰδίαν
they did   And   taking   them   He withdrew   privately

εἰς τόπον ἔρημον πόλεως καλουμένης Βηθσαϊδά. 11 οἱ δὲ ὄχλοι
to   a place deserted of a city   being called   Bethsaida.   the And crowds

γνόντες ἠκολούθησαν αὐτῷ· καὶ δεξάμενος αὐτούς, ἐλάλει
knowing   followed   Him. And having received them,   He spoke

αὐτοῖς περὶ τῆς βασιλείας τοῦ Θεοῦ, καὶ τοὺς χρείαν
to them   about the   kingdom   of God, and   those   need

ἔχοντας θεραπείας ἰᾶτο. 12 ἡ δὲ ἡμέρα ἤρξατο κλίνειν· προσ-
having   of healing He cured.   the But   day   began   to decline   coming

ελθόντες δὲ οἱ δώδεκα εἶπον αὐτῷ, Ἀπόλυσον τὸν ὄχλον,
up   And the twelve   said   to Him,   Let go   the   crowd

ἵνα ἀπελθόντες εἰς τὰς κύκλῳ κώμας καὶ τοὺς ἀγροὺς κατα-
that   going   into   the   around villages and the   farms   they

λύσωσι, καὶ εὕρωσιν ἐπισιτισμόν· ὅτι ὧδε ἐν ἐρήμῳ τόπῳ
may lodge   and may find   food supplies, because here in   deserted a place

ἐσμέν. 13 εἶπε δὲ πρὸς αὐτούς, Δότε αὐτοῖς ὑμεῖς φαγεῖν. οἱ δὲ
we are.   He said And to   them,   Give   them   You to eat. they But

εἶπον, Οὐκ εἰσὶν ἡμῖν πλεῖον ἢ πέντε ἄρτοι καὶ δύο ἰχθύες,
said,   Not is   to us more   than five   loaves   and two   fish,

εἰ μήτι πορευθέντες ἡμεῖς ἀγοράσωμεν εἰς πάντα τὸν λαὸν
if   not   going   we   may buy   for   all   people

τοῦτον βρώματα. 14 ἦσαν γὰρ ὡσεὶ ἄνδρες πεντακισχίλιοι.
this   foods.   there were For about   men   five thousand

εἶπε δὲ πρὸς τοὺς μαθητὰς αὐτοῦ, Κατακλίνατε αὐτοὺς
He said And to   the   disciples   of Him,   Cause to recline   them

King James Version (right column):

7. Now Herod the tetrarch heard of all that was done by him: and he was perplexed, because that it was said of some, that John was risen from the dead;

8 And of some, that Elias had appeared; and of others, that one of the old prophets was risen again.

9 And Herod said, John have I beheaded: but who is this, of whom I hear such things? And he desired to see him.

10. And the apostles, when they were returned, told him all that they had done. And he took them, and went aside privately into a desert place belonging to the city called Bethsaida.

11 And the people, when they knew (it), followed him: and he received them, and spake unto them of the kingdom of God, and healed them that had need of healing.

12. And when the day began to wear away, then came the twelve, and said unto him, Send the multitude away, that they may go into the towns and country round about, and lodge, and get victuals: for we are here in a desert place.

13 But he said unto them, Give ye them to eat. And they said, We have no more but five loaves and two fishes; except we should go and buy meat for all this people.

14 For they were about five thousand men. And he said to his disciples, Make them sit down

Literal Translation   **Luke 9:15**   *King James Version*

in groups, by fifties.
15 And they did so, and
made all recline.

2828   303   4004   2532 4160   3779 2532 347
κλισίας ἀνὰ πεντήκοντα. 15 καὶ ἐποίησαν οὕτω, καὶ ἀνέκλιναν
in groups by   fifties.   And they did   so, and made recline

by fifties in a company.
15 And they did so, and
made them all sit down.

16 And taking the five
loaves and the two fish,
looking up to Heaven,
He blessed them, and
broke, and gave to the
disciples to set before
the crowd.
17 And they ate and
were all filled. And
twelve hand baskets of
fragments of that left
over to them were taken
up.

537   2983 1161 3588 4002   740   2532 3588 1417 2486
ἅπαντας. 16 λαβὼν δὲ τοὺς πέντε ἄρτους καὶ τοὺς δύο ἰχθύας
all   taking And the five loaves and the two fish.

308   1519 3588 3772   2127   846   2532 2622
ἀναβλέψας εἰς τὸν οὐρανόν, εὐλόγησεν αὐτούς, καὶ κατέκλασε,
looking up to Heaven,   He blessed them,   and broke

2532 1325 3588 3101   3908   3588 3793   2532
καὶ ἐδίδου τοῖς μαθηταῖς παρατιθέναι τῷ ὄχλῳ. 17 καὶ
and gave to the disciples to set before the crowd.   And

5315 2532   5526   3956   2532 142 3588 4052
ἔφαγον καὶ ἐχορτάσθησαν πάντες· καὶ ἤρθη τὸ περισσεῦσαν
they ate and were filled   all.   And were taken the   excess

846   2801   2894   1427
αὐτοῖς κλασμάτων, κόφινοι δώδεκα.
to them of fragments hand-baskets twelve

16 Then he took the five
loaves and the two
fishes, and looking up to
heaven, he blessed
them, and brake, and
gave to the disciples to
set before the multitude.
17 And they did eat, and
were all filled: and there
was taken up of frag-
ments that remained to
them twelve baskets.

18. And it happened
(as) He was praying
alone, the disciples were
with Him. And He
questioned them, say-
ing, Whom do the
crowds say Me to be?
19 And answering, they
said, John the Baptist;
and others Elijah; and,
others that some
prophet of the ancients
has risen again.

2532 1096   1722 3588 1511 846   4336   2651
18. Καὶ ἐγένετο ἐν τῷ εἶναι αὐτὸν προσευχόμενον καταμόνας
And it happened (as) was Him   praying   alone,

4895   846 3588 3101   2532 1905   846   3004
συνῆσαν αὐτῷ οἱ μαθηταί· καὶ ἐπηρώτησεν αὐτούς, λέγων,
were with Him the disciples And He questioned them,   saying,

5101 3165 3004   3588 3793 1511   3588 1161   611   2036
Τίνα με λέγουσιν οἱ ὄχλοι εἶναι; 19 οἱ δὲ ἀποκριθέντες εἶπον,
Whom Me say   the crowds to be?   they And answering   said,

2491   3588 910   243   1161 2243   243 1161 3754
Ἰωάννην τὸν βαπτιστήν· ἄλλοι δὲ Ἡλίαν· ἄλλοι δὲ, ὅτι
John   the Baptist;   others but Elijah; others and that

4396   5100 3588 744   450   2036 1161 846   5210
προφήτης τις τῶν ἀρχαίων ἀνέστη. 20 εἶπε δὲ αὐτοῖς, Ὑμεῖς
a prophet certain of the ancients rose again. He said And to them,   you

18. And it came to pass,
as he was alone praying,
his disciples were with
him: and he asked them,
saying, Whom say the
people that I am?
19 They answering
said, John the Baptist;
but some (say), Elias;
and others (say), that
one of the old prophets
is risen again.

20 And He said to them,
But whom do you say
Me to be? And answer-
ing, Peter said, The
Christ of God.

1161 5101 3165 3004 1511   611   1161 3588 4074 2036 3588
δὲ τίνα με λέγετε εἶναι; ἀποκριθεὶς δὲ ὁ Πέτρος εἶπε, Τὸν
And, whom Me say   to be? answering And the Peter said, The

5547   3588 2316   3588 1161 2008   846   3853
Χριστὸν τοῦ Θεοῦ. 21 ὁ δὲ ἐπιτιμήσας αὐτοῖς παρήγγειλε
Christ   of God. He But warning   them   ordered

20 He said unto them,
But whom say ye that I
am? Peter answering
said, The Christ of God.

21 And strictly warning
them, He ordered no
one to tell this,
22 saying, It behoves
the Son of man to suffer
many things and be re-
jected by the elders and
chief priests and
scribes, and be killed,
and be raised the third
day.

3367 2036 5124   2036 3754 1163 3588 5207 3588   444
μηδενὶ εἰπεῖν τοῦτο, 22 εἰπὼν ὅτι Δεῖ τὸν υἱὸν τοῦ ἀνθρώπου
no one to tell this,   saying, that it behoves the Son of man

4183   3958 2532   593   575 3588   4245
πολλὰ παθεῖν, καὶ ἀποδοκιμασθῆναι ἀπὸ τῶν πρεσβυτέρων
many things to suffer, and to be rejected   from the   elders

2532 749   2532   1122   2532   615   2532 3588
καὶ ἀρχιερέων καὶ γραμματέων, καὶ ἀποκτανθῆναι, καὶ τῇ
and chief priests and scribes,   and to be killed,   and the

21 And he straitly
charged them, and
commanded (them) to
tell no man that thing;
22 Saying, The Son of
man must suffer many
things, and be rejected
of the elders and chief
priests and scribes, and
be slain, and be raised
the third day.

23. And He said to all,
If anyone desires to
come after Me, let him
deny himself and take
up his cross daily. And
let him follow Me.

24. For whoever desires
to save his life, he will
lose it. But whoever
may lose his life for My
sake, this one will save
it.

5154   2250   1453   3004 1161 4314 3956   1487 5100
τρίτῃ ἡμέρᾳ ἐγερθῆναι. 23 Ἔλεγε δὲ πρὸς πάντας, Εἴ τις
third   day   to be raised   He said And to   all,   If anyone

2309 3694 3450 2064   533   1438   2532 142
θέλει ὀπίσω μου ἐλθεῖν, ἀπαρνησάσθω ἑαυτόν, καὶ ἀράτω
desires after Me to come, let him deny   himself, and take up

3588 4716   846 2596 2250 2532 190   3427 3739
τὸν σταυρὸν αὐτοῦ καθ' ἡμέραν, καὶ ἀκολουθείτω μοι. 24 ὃς
the cross   of him day by day. And let him follow Me. whoever

1063 302 2309 3588 5590   846   4982   622   846   3739
γὰρ ἂν θέλῃ τὴν ψυχὴν αὐτοῦ σῶσαι, ἀπολέσει αὐτήν· ὃς
For may desire the life   of him to save, he will lose it whoever

1161 302 622   3588 5590   846   1752 1700 3778   4982
δ' ἂν ἀπολέσῃ τὴν ψυχὴν αὐτοῦ ἕνεκεν ἐμοῦ, οὗτος σώσει
But may lose   the life   of him for the sake of Me, this one will save

23. And he said to
(them) all, If any (man)
will come after me, let
him deny himself, and
take up his cross daily,
and follow me.

24 For whosoever will
save his life shall lose it:
but whosoever will lose
his life for my sake, the
same shall save it.

Literal Translation	Greek (interlinear, with Strong's numbers)	King James Version
25 For what is a man profited gaining the whole world, but destroying himself or suffering loss?	846 5101 1063 5623 444 2770 3588 2889 αὐτήν. 25 τί γάρ ὠφελεῖται ἄνθρωπος, κερδήσας τὸν κόσμον it what For is profited a man gaining the world 3650 1438 1161 622 2228 2210 3739 1063 302 ὅλον, ἑαυτὸν δὲ ἀπολέσας ἢ ζημιωθείς; 26 ὃς γὰρ ἂν whole, himself but destroying or suffering loss? whoever for may	25 For what is a man advantaged, if he gain the whole world, and lose himself, or be cast away?
26 For whoever may be ashamed of Me and My words, the Son of man will be ashamed of that one when He comes in His glory, and (that) of the Father, and of the holy angels.	1870 3165 2532 3588 1699 3056 5126 3588 5207 3588 ἐπαισχυνθῇ με καὶ τοὺς ἐμοὺς λόγους, τοῦτον ὁ υἱὸς τοῦ be ashamed of Me and the of Me words, this one the Son 444 1870 3752 2064 1722 3588 1391 846 2532 ἀνθρώπου ἐπαισχυνθήσεται, ὅταν ἔλθῃ ἐν τῇ δόξῃ αὐτοῦ καὶ of man will be ashamed of when He comes in the glory of Him, and 3588 3962 2532 3588 40 32 3004 1161 5213 230 τοῦ πατρὸς καὶ τῶν ἁγίων ἀγγέλων. 27 λέγω δὲ ὑμῖν ἀληθῶς, of the Father, and of the holy angels. I say But to You truly	26 For whosoever shall be ashamed of me and of my words, of him shall the Son of man be ashamed, when he shall come in his own glory, and (in his) Father's, and of the holy angels.
27 But truly I say to you, There are some of those standing here who in no way shall taste of death until they see the kingdom of God.	1526 5100 3588 5602 2476 3739 3756 3361 1089 2288 εἰσί τινες τῶν ὧδε ἑστηκότων, οἳ οὐ μὴ γεύσονται θανάτου, are some of those here standing who in no way shall taste of death 2193 302 1492 3588 932 3588 2316 ἕως ἂν ἴδωσι τὴν βασιλείαν τοῦ Θεοῦ. until may they see the kingdom of God	27 But I tell you of a truth, there be some standing here, which shall not taste of death, till they see the kingdom of God.
28. And about eight days after these sayings, it happened also taking Peter and John and James, He went into the mountain to pray.	1096 1161 3326 3588 3056 5128 5616 2250 3638 28. Ἐγένετο δὲ μετὰ τοὺς λόγους τούτους ὡσεὶ ἡμέραι ὀκτώ, it was And after sayings these, about days eight, 2532 3880 3588 4074 2532 2491 2532 2385 καὶ παραλαβὼν τὸν Πέτρον καὶ Ἰωάννην καὶ Ἰάκωβον, also taking Peter and John and James	28. And it came to pass about an eight days after these sayings, he took Peter and John and James, and went up into a mountain to pray.
29 And in His praying, the appearance of His face became different, and His clothing (was) dazzling white	305 1519 3588 3735 4336 2532 1096 1722 3588 ἀνέβη εἰς τὸ ὄρος προσεύξασθαι. 29 καὶ ἐγένετο ἐν τῷ He went into the mountain to pray. And it came to be in the 4336 846 3588 1491 3588 4383 846 2087 προσεύχεσθαι αὐτὸν τὸ εἶδος τοῦ προσώπου αὐτοῦ ἕτερον, praying of Him the appearance of the face of Him different	29 And as he prayed, the fashion of his countenance was altered, and his raiment (was) white (and) glistering.
30 And, behold, two men talked with Him, who were Moses and Elijah,	2532 3588 2441 846 3022 1823 2532 2400 καὶ ὁ ἱματισμὸς αὐτοῦ λευκὸς ἐξαστράπτων. 30 καὶ ἰδού, and the clothing of Him white dazzling And behold! 435 1417 4814 846 3748 2258 3475 2532 ἄνδρες δύο συνελάλουν αὐτῷ, οἵτινες ἦσαν Μωσῆς καὶ men Two talked with Him, who were Moses and	30 And, behold, there talked with him two men, which were Moses and Elias:
31 who appearing in glory, (they) spoke of His exodus, which He was about to fulfill in Jerusalem.	2243 3739 3700 1722 1391 3004 3588 1841 846 3739 Ἠλίας. 31 οἱ ὀφθέντες ἐν δόξῃ ἔλεγον τὴν ἔξοδον αὐτοῦ ἦν Elijah, who appearing in glory spoke of the exodus of Him, which 3195 4137 1722 2419 3588 1161 4074 2532 3588 4862 846 ἔμελλε πληροῦν ἐν Ἱερουσαλήμ. 32 ὁ δὲ Πέτρος καὶ οἱ σὺν αὐτῷ He was about to fulfill in Jerusalem. And Peter and those with Him	31 Who appeared in glory, and spake of his decease which he should accomplish at Jerusalem.
32 But Peter and those with him were pressed down with sleep. But fully awakening, they saw His glory, and the two men standing with Him.	2258 916 5258 1235 1161 1492 3588 ἦσαν βεβαρημένοι ὕπνῳ· διαγρηγορήσαντες δὲ εἶδον τὴν were being pressed down with sleep awakening fully) But they saw the 1391 846 2532 3588 1417 435 3588 4921 846 δόξαν αὐτοῦ, καὶ τοὺς δύο ἄνδρας τοὺς συνεστῶτας αὐτῷ. glory of Him, and the two men standing with Him.	32 But Peter and they that were with him were heavy with sleep: and when they were awake, they saw his glory, and the two men that stood with him.
33 And it happened in their departing from Him, Peter said to Jesus, Master, it is good for (us) to be here. And, Let us make three tents, one for You, and one for Moses, and one for Elijah, not knowing what he said.	2532 1096 1722 3588 1316 846 575 846 2036 33 καὶ ἐγένετο, ἐν τῷ διαχωρίζεσθαι αὐτοὺς ἀπ' αὐτοῦ, εἶπεν And it happened in the departing of them from Him,, said 3588 4074 4314 588 2424 1988 2570 2076 2248 ὁ Πέτρος πρὸς τὸν Ἰησοῦν, Ἐπιστάτα, καλόν ἐστιν ἡμᾶς Peter to Jesus, Master, good it is us 5602 1511 2532 4160 4633 5140 3391 4671 2532 ὧδε εἶναι· καὶ ποιήσωμεν σκηνὰς τρεῖς, μίαν σοί, καὶ here to be, and us make tents three, one for You, and 3475 3391 2532 3391 2243 3361 1492 3739 3004 5023 1161 Μωσεῖ μίαν, καὶ μίαν Ἠλίᾳ· μὴ εἰδὼς ὃ λέγει. 34 ταῦτα δὲ Moses one, and one for Elijah, not knowing what he says these things And	33 And it came to pass, as they departed from him, Peter said unto Jesus, Master, it is good for us to be here: and let us make three tabernacles; one for thee, and one for Moses, and one for Elias: not knowing what he said.
34 And he saying these things,		34 While he thus spake,

Literal Translation	Greek / Interlinear	King James Version
a cloud came and overshadowed them. And they feared (as) those entered into the cloud.	846 3004 1096 3507 2532 1982 846 αὐτοῦ λέγοντος, ἐγένετο νεφέλη καὶ ἐπεσκίασεν αὐτούς· him saying, came a cloud and overshadowed them, 5399 1161 1722 3588 1565 1525 1519 3588 3507 ἐφοβήθησαν δὲ ἐν τῷ ἐκείνους εἰσελθεῖν εἰς τὴν νεφέλην. they feared and in the of those entering into the cloud.	there came a cloud, and overshadowed them: and they feared as they entered into the cloud.
35 And a voice came out of the cloud, saying. This is My Son, the Beloved, hear Him! (Ps. 2:7; Deut. 18:15)	2532 5456 1096 1537 3588 3507 3004 3778 2076 3588 35 καὶ φωνὴ ἐγένετο ἐκ τῆς νεφέλης λέγουσα, Οὗτός ἐστιν ὁ And a voice came out of the cloud, saying, This is the 5207 3450 3588 27 846 191 2532 1722 3588 1096 3588 υἱός μου ὁ ἀγαπητός αὐτοῦ ἀκούετε. 36 καὶ ἐν τῷ γενέσθαι τὴν Son of Me, the Beloved, Him hear. And in the occurring of the	35 And there came a voice out of the cloud, saying, This is my beloved Son: hear him.
36 And as the voice occurred, Jesus was found alone. And they were quiet. And (they) reported to no one in those days, nothing which they had seen	5456 2147 3588 2424 3441 2532 846 4601 2532 φωνὴν, εὑρέθη ὁ Ἰησοῦς μόνος. καὶ αὐτοὶ ἐσίγησαν, καὶ voice, was found Jesus alone. And they were quiet, and 3762 518 1722 1565 3588 2250 3762 3739 οὐδενὶ ἀπήγγειλαν ἐν ἐκείναις ταῖς ἡμέραις οὐδὲν ὧν to no one reported in those days, nothing which 3708 ἑωράκασιν. they had seen.	36 And when the voice was past, Jesus was found alone. And they kept (it) close, and told no man in those days any of those things which they had seen.
37. And it happened on the next day, they coming down from the mountain, a large crowd met Him	1096 1161 1722 3588 1836 2250 2718 846 575 37. Ἐγένετο δὲ ἐν τῇ ἑξῆς ἡμέρᾳ, κατελθόντων αὐτῶν ἀπὸ it was And in the next day, coming down them from 3588 3735 4876 846 3793 4183 2532 2400 435 τοῦ ὄρους, συνήντησεν αὐτῷ ὄχλος πολύς. 38 καὶ ἰδού, ἀνήρ the mountain. met Him a crowd large. And, behold! A man	37. And it came to pass, that on the next day, when they were come down from the hill, much people met him.
38. And, behold! A man called aloud from the crowd, saying, Teacher, I beg You to look upon my son, because he is my only born.	575 3588 3793 310 3004 1320 1189 4675 ἀπὸ τοῦ ὄχλου ἀνέβόησε, λέγων, Διδάσκαλε, δέομαί σου, from the crowd cried out, saying, Teacher, I beg You 1914 1909 3588 5207 3450 3754 3439 2076 3427 2532 ἐπιβλέψον ἐπὶ τὸν υἱόν μου, ὅτι μονογενής ἐστί μοι. 39 καὶ to look upon the son of me, because only born he is of me. And	38. And, behold, a man of the company cried out, saying, Master, I beseech thee, look upon my son: for he is mine only child.
39. And, behold! A spirit takes hold of him, and (he) suddenly cries out, and (it) convulses him, with foam. And (it) departs from him with difficulty, bruising him.	2400 4151 2983 846 2532 1810 2896 2532 ἰδού, πνεῦμα λαμβάνει αὐτόν, καὶ ἐξαίφνης κράζει, καὶ behold! A spirit takes hold of him, and suddenly he cries out, and 672 846 3326 876 2532 3425 672 575 σπαράσσει αὐτὸν μετὰ ἀφροῦ, καὶ μόγις ἀποχωρεῖ ἀπ' convulses him with foam, and with difficulty departs from	39. And, lo, a spirit taketh him, and he suddenly crieth out; and it teareth him that he foameth again, and bruising him hardly departeth from him.
40. And I begged Your disciples, that they cast it out. And they were not able.	846 4937 846 2532 1189 3588 3101 4675 αὐτοῦ, συντρίβων αὐτόν. 40 καὶ ἐδεήθην τῶν μαθητῶν σου him, bruising him. And I begged the disciples of You 2443 1544 846 2532 3756 1410 611 1161 ἵνα ἐκβάλλωσιν αὐτό, καὶ οὐκ ἠδυνήθησαν. 41 ἀποκριθεὶς δὲ ὁ that they cast out it, and not they were able. answering And	40. And I besought thy disciples to cast him out; and they could not.
41. And answering, Jesus said, O unbelieving and being perverted generation, until when shall I be with you and endure you? Bring your son here.	3588 2424 2036 5599 1074 571 2532 1294 2193 ὁ Ἰησοῦς εἶπεν, Ὦ γενεὰ ἄπιστος καὶ διεστραμμένη, ἕως Jesus said, O generation unbelieving and being perverted, until 4219 2071 4314 5209 2532 430 5216 4317 πότε ἔσομαι πρὸς ὑμᾶς, καὶ ἀνέξομαι ὑμῶν; προσάγαγε when shall I be with you and endure you? Bring	41. And Jesus answering said, O faithless and perverse generation, how long shall I be with you, and suffer you? Bring thy son hither.
42. But (he) yet coming near, the demon tore him and violently convulsed (him). But Jesus rebuked the unclean spirit, and healed the child, and gave him back to his father.	5602 3588 5207 4675 2089 1161 4334 846 4486 ὧδε τὸν υἱόν σου. 42 ἔτι δὲ προσερχομένου αὐτοῦ, ἔρρηξεν here the son of you yet But coming near him. tore 846 3588 1140 2532 4952 2008 1161 3588 ὁ αὐτὸν τὸ δαιμόνιον καὶ συνεσπάραξεν· ἐπετίμησε δὲ ὁ him the demon and violently convulsed. rebuked But 2424 3588 4151 3588 169 2532 2390 3588 3816 Ἰησοῦς τῷ πνεύματι τῷ ἀκαθάρτῳ, καὶ ἰάσατο τὸν παῖδα, Jesus the spirit the unclean, and healed the child,	42. And as he was yet a coming, the devil threw him down, and tare (him) And Jesus rebuked the unclean spirit, and healed the child, and delivered him again to his father.
43. And all were astounded	2532 591 846 3588 3962 846 1605 1161 καὶ ἀπέδωκεν αὐτὸν τῷ πατρὶ αὐτοῦ. 43 ἐξεπλήσσοντο δὲ and gave back him to the father of him were astounded And	43. And they were all amazed

Literal Translation	Greek Interlinear	King James Version
at the majesty of God. And (as) all (were) marveling at all things which He did, Jesus said to His disciples.	3956 1909 3588 3168 3588 2316. πάντες ἐπὶ τῇ μεγαλειότητι τοῦ Θεοῦ. all at the majesty of God. 3956 1161 2296 1909 3956 3739 4160 3588 Πάντων δὲ θαυμαζόντων ἐπὶ πᾶσιν οἷς ἐποίησεν ὁ all And marveling at all things which He did, 2424 2036 4314 3588 3101 846 5087 5210 1519 3588 Ἰησοῦς, εἶπε πρὸς τοὺς μαθητὰς αὐτοῦ, 44 Θέσθε ὑμεῖς εἰς τὰ Jesus said to the disciples of Him, Lay you into the	at the mighty power of God. But while they wondered every one at all things which Jesus did, he said unto his disciples,
44 You lay into your ears these sayings, for the Son of man is about to be betrayed into (the) hands of men.	3775 5216 3588 3056 5128 3588 1063 5207 3588 444 ὦτα ὑμῶν τοὺς λόγους τούτους· ὁ γὰρ υἱὸς τοῦ ἀνθρώπου ears of you words these. the For Son of man 3195 3860 1519 5495 444 3588 1161 50 μέλλει παραδίδοσθαι εἰς χεῖρας ἀνθρώπων. 45 οἱ δὲ ἠγνόουν is about to be betrayed into (the) hands of men. they But knew not	44 Let these sayings sink down into your ears: for the Son of man shall be delivered into the hands of men.
45 But they did not know this Word, and it was veiled from them so that they not perceive it. And they feared to ask Him about this Word.	3588 4487 5124 2532 2258 3871 575 846 2443 τὸ ῥῆμα τοῦτο, καὶ ἦν παρακεκαλυμμένον ἀπ' αὐτῶν, ἵνα Word this. and it was being veiled from them, so that 3361 143 846 2532 5399 2065 846 4012 μὴ αἴσθωνται αὐτό· καὶ ἐφοβοῦντο ἐρωτῆσαι αὐτὸν περὶ not they perceive it. And they feared to ask Him about 3588 4487 5127 τοῦ ῥήματος τούτου. Word this.	45 But they understood not this saying, and it was hid from them, that they perceived it not: and they feared to ask him of that saying.
46. But a reasoning came in among them, who might be (the) greater of them. 47 And seeing the reasoning of their heart, laying hold of a child, Jesus stood it beside Himself,	1525 1161 1261 1722 846 3588 5101 302 1498 3187 46. Εἰσῆλθε δὲ διαλογισμὸς ἐν αὐτοῖς, τὸ τίς ἂν εἴη μείζων came in But a reasoning among them, who might be greater 846 3588 1161 2424 1492 3588 1261 3588 2588 αὐτῶν. 47 ὁ δὲ Ἰησοῦς ἰδὼν τὸν διαλογισμὸν τῆς καρδίας of them. And Jesus having seen the reasoning of the heart 846 1949 3813 2476 846 3844 1438 αὐτῶν, ἐπιλαβόμενος παιδίον, ἔστησεν αὐτὸ παρ' ἑαυτῷ, of them, having laid hold of a child, stood it beside Himself,	46. Then there arose a reasoning among them, which of them should be greatest. 47 And Jesus, perceiving the thought of their heart, took a child, and set him by him,
48 and said to them, Whoever receives this child on My name receives Me. And whoever receives Me receives the (One) who has sent Me. For the one being lesser among you all, this one shall be great.	2532 2036 846 3739 1437 1209 5124 3588 3813 1909 3588 48 καὶ εἶπεν αὐτοῖς, Ὃς ἐὰν δέξηται τοῦτο τὸ παιδίον ἐπὶ τῷ and said to them, Whoever receives this child on the 3686 3450 1691 1209 2532 3739 1437 1691 1209 1209 3588 ὀνόματί μου ἐμὲ δέχεται· καὶ ὃς ἐὰν ἐμὲ δέξηται δέχεται τὸν name of Me, Me receives. And whoever receives Me receives the (One) 649 3165 3588 1063 3398 1722 3956 5213 5225 ἀποστείλαντά με· ὁ γὰρ μικρότερος ἐν πᾶσιν ὑμῖν ὑπάρχων having sent Me. the For lesser among all you being, 3778 2071 3173 οὗτός ἔσται μέγας. this one will be great.	48 And said unto them, Whosoever shall receive this child in my name receiveth me: and whosoever shall receive me receiveth him that sent me: for he that is least among you all, the same shall be great.
49 And answering, John said, Master, we saw someone casting out demons on Your name, and we stopped him because he does not follow with us. 50 And Jesus said to them, Do not stop (them) for whoever is not against us is for us.	611 1161 3588 2491 2036 1988 1492 5100 49. Ἀποκριθεὶς δὲ ὁ Ἰωάννης εἶπεν, Ἐπιστάτα, εἴδομέν τινα answering And John said, Master, we saw someone 1909 3588 3686 4675 1544 3588 1140 2532 ἐπὶ τῷ ὀνόματί σου ἐκβάλλοντα τὰ δαιμόνια· καὶ on the Name of You casting out demons, and 2967 846 3754 3756 190 3326 2257 2532 2036 ἐκωλύσαμεν αὐτὸν, ὅτι οὐκ ἀκολουθεῖ μεθ' ἡμῶν. 50 καὶ εἶπε stopped him, because not he follows with us. And said 4314 846 3588 2424 3361 2967 3739 1063 3756 2076 2596 πρὸς αὐτὸν ὁ Ἰησοῦς, Μὴ κωλύετε, ὃς γὰρ οὐκ ἔστι καθ' to them Jesus, Not do stop (them), whoever for not is against 2257 5228 2257 2076 ἡμῶν ὑπὲρ ἡμῶν ἐστιν. us for us is	49 And John answered and said, Master, we saw one casting out devils in thy name; and we forbad him, because he followeth not with us. 50 And Jesus said unto him, Forbid (him) not: for he that is not against us is for us.
51. And it happened in the fulfilling (of) the days of His	1096 1161 1722 3588 4845 3588 2250 3588 51. Ἐγένετο δὲ ἐν τῷ συμπληροῦσθαι τὰς ἡμέρας τῆς it happened And in the fulfilling of the days of the	51. And it came to pass, when the time was come that he

Literal Translation   **Luke 9:52**   *King James Version*

354   846   2532   846   3588   4383   846   4741
ἀναλήψεως αὐτοῦ, καὶ αὐτὸς τὸ πρόσωπον αὐτοῦ ἐστήριξε

taking up, even He set | taking up of Him, even He the face of Him set | should be received up,
His face to go to Jerusa- | | he stedfastly set his face
lem. | 3588   4198   1519   2419   2532   649   32 | to go to Jerusalem,
| τοῦ πορεύεσθαι εἰς Ἰερουσαλήμ, 52 καὶ ἀπέστειλεν ἀγγέλους |
52 And (He) sent mes- | to go to Jerusalem. And (He) sent messengers | **52** And sent messen-
sengers before His face. | 4253   4383   846   2532   4198   1525   1519   2968 | gers before his face: and
And going they went | πρὸ προσώπου αὐτοῦ· καὶ πορευθέντες εἰσῆλθον εἰς κώμην | they went, and entered
into a village of Samari- | before the face of Him. And going they went into a village | into a village of the Sa-
tans, so as to make | | maritans, to make ready
ready for Him. | 4541   5620   2090   846   2532 3756 1209   846 | for him.
53 And they did not re- | Σαμαρειτῶν, ὥστε ἑτοιμάσαι αὐτῷ· 53 καὶ οὐκ ἐδέξαντο αὐτόν, | **53** And they did not re-
ceive Him, because His | of Samaritans, so as to make ready for Him. And not they received Him. | ceive him, because his
face was going toward | 3754 3588   4383   846   2258   4198   1519   2419 | face was as though he
Jerusalem. | ὅτι τὸ πρόσωπον αὐτοῦ ἦν πορευόμενον εἰς Ἰερουσαλήμ. | would go to Jerusalem.
| because the face of Him was going to Jerusalem. |

1492   1161 3588 3101   846   2385   2532   2491   2036
54 ἰδόντες δὲ οἱ μαθηταὶ αὐτοῦ Ἰάκωβος καὶ Ἰωάννης εἶπον,

54 And seeing, His dis- | seeing And the disciples of Him, James and John said, | **54** And when his disci-
ciples James and John | 2962   2309   2036   4442   2597   575 3588   3772   2532 | ples James and John
said, Lord, do You de- | Κύριε, θέλεις εἴπωμεν πῦρ καταβῆναι ἀπὸ τοῦ οὐρανοῦ, καὶ | saw (this), they said,
sire (that) we tell fire to | Lord, do You desire (that) we tell fire to come down from Heaven and | Lord, wilt thou that we
come down from | | command fire to come
Heaven, and to destroy | 355   846   5613 2532 2243   4160   4762   1161 | down from heaven, and
them even as Elijah did? | ἀναλῶσαι αὐτούς, ὡς καὶ Ἡλίας ἐποίησε; 55 στραφεὶς δὲ | consume them, even as
(2 K. 1:10-12) | to destroy them, as also Elijah did? turning But | Elias did?
55 But turning He re- | | **55** But he turned, and
buked them. And He | 2008   846   2532 2036   3756   1492   3634   4151 | rebuked them, and said,
said, You do not know | ἐπετίμησεν αὐτοῖς, καὶ εἶπεν, Οὐκ οἴδατε οἵου πνεύματός | Ye know not what man-
of what spirit you are. | He rebuked them. and said, Not you know of what spirit | ner of spirit ye are of.

2075   5210   3588 1063 5207   3588   444   3756 2064   5590
ἐστε ὑμεῖς· 56 ὁ γὰρ υἱὸς τοῦ ἀνθρώπου οὐκ ἦλθε ψυχὰς

56 For the Son of man | are you. the For Son of man not did come the souls | **56** For the Son of man is
did not come to destroy | 444   622   235   4982   2532   4198   1519 | not come to destroy
men's souls, but to save. | ἀνθρώπων ἀπολέσαι, ἀλλὰ σῶσαι. καὶ ἐπορεύθησαν εἰς | men's lives, but to save
And they went to an- | of men to destroy, but to save. And they went to | (them). And they went
other village. | | to another village.

2087   2968
ἑτέραν κώμην.

another village

1096   1161   4198   846   1722 3588 3598 2036 5100 4314
57. Ἐγένετο δὲ πορευομένων αὐτῶν ἐν τῇ ὁδῷ, εἶπέ τις πρὸς

57. And it happened | it happened And, going them in the way, said one to | **57.** And it came to pass,
(as) they (were) going in | 846   190   4671 3699 302   565   2962   2532 2036 | that, as they went in the
the way, one said to | αὐτόν, Ἀκολουθήσω σοι ὅπου ἂν ἀπέρχῃ, Κύριε 58 καὶ εἶπεν | way, a certain (man)
Him, I will follow You | Him, I will follow You wherever may You go, Lord. And said | said unto him, Lord, I
everywhere You may | | will follow thee whith-
go, Lord. | 846 3588 2424   3588   258   5454   2192   2532 3588 | ersoever thou goest.
58 And Jesus said to | αὐτῷ ὁ Ἰησοῦς, Αἱ ἀλώπεκες φωλεοὺς ἔχουσι, καὶ τὰ | **58** And Jesus said unto
him, The foxes have | to Him Jesus, The foxes holes have, and the | him, Foxes have holes,
holes, and the birds of | 4071   3588   3772   2682   3588 1161 5207 3588   444 | and birds of the air
the heaven nests, but the | πετεινὰ τοῦ οὐρανοῦ κατασκηνώσεις· ὁ δὲ υἱὸς τοῦ ἀνθρώπου | (have) nests; but the
Son of man has no- | birds of the heaven nests; the but Son of man | Son of man hath not
where He may lay (His) | | where to lay (his) head.
head. | 3756 2192 4226 3588   2776   2827   2036 1161 4314   2087 |
| οὐκ ἔχει ποῦ τὴν κεφαλὴν κλίνῃ. 59 εἶπε δὲ πρὸς ἕτερον, |
59 And He said to an- | not has where the head He may lay. He said And to another, | **59** And he said unto an-
other, Follow Me. But | 190   3427 3588 1161 2036   2962   2010   3427   565 | other, Follow me. But
he said, Lord, allow me | Ἀκολούθει μοι. ὁ δὲ εἶπε, Κύριε, ἐπίτρεψόν μοι ἀπελθόντι | he said, Lord, suffer me
to go first to bury my fa- | Follow Me. he But said, Lord, allow me having gone | first to go and bury my
ther. | | father.
| 4412   2290   3588   3962   3450   2036 1161 846   3588   2424 |
| πρῶτον θάψαι τὸν πατέρα μου. 60 εἶπε δὲ αὐτῷ, ὁ Ἰησοῦς |
60 But Jesus said to | first to bury the father of me. said But to him, Jesus, | **60** Jesus said unto him,
him, Leave the dead to | 863   3588   3498   2290   3588   1438   3498   4771 1161 | Let the dead bury their
bury their dead, but go- | Ἄφες τοὺς νεκροὺς θάψαι τοὺς ἑαυτῶν νεκρούς· σὺ δὲ | dead: but go thou and
ing out, you announce | Leave the dead to bury the of themselves dead, you but | preach the kingdom of
the kingdom of God. | | God.
| 565   1229   3588   932   3588   2316   2036 1161 2532 |
| ἀπελθὼν διάγγελλε τὴν βασιλείαν τοῦ Θεοῦ. 61 εἶπε δὲ καὶ |
61 And also another | going out announce the kingdom of God. said And also | **61** And another also
said. | | said,

Literal Translation	Luke 9:62	King James Version
I will follow You, Lord, but first allow me to take leave of those in my house. 62 But Jesus said to him, No one putting his hand on the plow, and looking at the things behind, is fit for the kingdom of God.	2087 190 4671 2962 4412 1161 2010 3427 ἕτερος, Ἀκολουθήσω σοι, Κύριε· πρῶτον δὲ ἐπίτρεψόν μοι another. I will follow You, Lord, first but allow me 657 3588 1519 3588 3624 3450 2036 1161 4314 846 3588 ἀποτάξασθαι τοῖς εἰς τὸν οἶκόν μου. 62 εἶπε δὲ πρὸς αὐτὸν ὁ to take leave of those in the house of me. 62 said But to him 2424 3762 1911 3588 5495 846 1909 723 Ἰησοῦς, Οὐδεὶς, ἐπιβαλὼν τὴν χεῖρα αὐτοῦ ἐπ' ἄροτρον Jesus, No one putting the hand of him on the plow 2532 991 1519 3588 3694 2111 2076 1519 3588 932 καὶ βλέπων εἰς τὰ ὀπίσω, εὔθετός ἐστιν εἰς τὴν βασιλείαν and looking to the things behind fit is for the kingdom 3588 2316 τοῦ Θεοῦ. of God.	Lord, I will follow thee; but let me first go bid them farewell, which are at home at my house. 62 And Jesus said unto him, No man, having put his hand to the plough, and looking back, is fit for the kingdom of God.

Acrostic Index

The following is the full chapter, in English and in Greek of John: Chapter 4, Verse 5, where acrostic 6 begins, is clearly marked.

1. Then when the Lord knew that the Pharisees heard that Jesus was making more disciples and baptizing (more) than John.

2 though truly Jesus Himself did not baptize, but His disciples.

3 He left Judea and went away into Galilee again.

4. And it was needful for Him to pass through Samaria.

5 And He came to a Samaritan city being called Sychar, near the piece of land Jacob had given to his son Joseph.

6 And Jacob's fountain was there. Then being wearied by the journey, Jesus was sitting thus on the fountain. (It) was about (the) sixth hour.

7 A woman came out of Samaria to draw water. Jesus said to her, Give Me (some) to drink.
8 For His disciples had gone away into the city that they might buy provisions.
9 Then the Samaritan woman said to Him, How do you, being a Jew, ask to drink from me, (I) being a Samaritan woman? For Jews do not have dealings with Samaritans.

10 Jesus answered and said to her, If you knew the gift of God, and who is the (One) saying

---

5613   3767 1097 3588 2962   3754   191   3588 5330   3754
1. Ὡς οὖν ἔγνω ὁ Κύριος, ὅτι ἤκουσαν οἱ Φαρισαῖοι ὅτι
   as Then knew the Lord   that heard   the Pharisees that
2424   4119   3101   4160 2532   2228   2491
Ἰησοῦς πλείονας μαθητὰς ποιεῖ καὶ βαπτίζει ἢ Ἰωάννης
Jesus   more   disciples making and baptizing than John

2544   2424   846 3756   907   235   3588   3101
2 καίτοιγε Ἰησοῦς αὐτὸς οὐκ ἐβάπτιζεν, ἀλλ' οἱ μαθηταὶ
  though   Jesus Himself not baptized, but the disciples
846   863   3588   2449   2532 565   3825 1519 3588
αὐτοῦ, 3 ἀφῆκε τὴν Ἰουδαίαν, καὶ ἀπῆλθε πάλιν εἰς τὴν
of Him, He left the Judea   and went away again   into
1056   1163 1161 846   1330   1223 3588   4540
Γαλιλαίαν. 4 ἔδει δὲ αὐτὸν διέρχεσθαι διὰ τῆς Σαμαρείας.
Galilee.   it behoved And Him   to pass   through Samaria.

2064   3767 1519 4172 3588   4540   3004   4965
5 Ἔρχεται οὖν εἰς πόλιν τῆς Σαμαρείας λεγομένην Συχάρ,
  He comes Then into a city of Samaria being called Sychar,
4139   3588 5564 3739 1325   2384   2501 3588 5207 846
πλησίον τοῦ χωρίου ὃ ἔδωκεν Ἰακὼβ Ἰωσὴφ τῷ υἱῷ αὐτοῦ·
near   the piece of land that had given Jacob to Joseph the son of him.

2258 1161 1563 4077 3588   2384 3588 3767 2424   2872   1537 3588
6 ἦν δὲ ἐκεῖ πηγὴ τοῦ Ἰακώβ. ὁ οὖν Ἰησοῦς κεκοπιακὼς ἐκ τῆς
was And there a fountain of Jacob. Then Jesus being wearied from the
3597   2516   3779   1909 3588 4077   5610 2258 5616
ὁδοιπορίας ἐκαθέζετο οὕτως ἐπὶ τῇ πηγῇ. ὥρα ἦν ὡσεὶ
journey   was, sitting thus   on the well, (the) hour was about
1623   2064   1135 1537 3588   4540   501   5204   3004
ἕκτη. 7 Ἔρχεται γυνὴ ἐκ τῆς Σαμαρείας ἀντλῆσαι ὕδωρ· λέγει
(the) sixth comes   A woman of Samaria   to draw   water. says
846 3588 2424   1325 3427 4095   3588 1063 3101   846   565
αὐτῇ ὁ Ἰησοῦς, Δός μοι πιεῖν. 8 οἱ γὰρ μαθηταὶ αὐτοῦ ἀπελη-
to her, Jesus, Give Me to drink. the For disciples of Him had gone
1519 3588 4172   2443 5160   59   3004   3767
λύθεισαν εἰς τὴν πόλιν, ἵνα τροφὰς ἀγοράσωσι. 9 λέγει οὖν
away   into the city,   that foods   they might buy says Then
846 3588 1135 3588   4542   4459 4771   2453   5607 3844   1700
αὐτῷ ἡ γυνὴ ἡ Σαμαρεῖτις, Πῶς σὺ Ἰουδαῖος ὢν παρ' ἐμοῦ
to Him the woman the Samaria, How do you, a Jew   being, from me
4095 154   5607   1135   4542   3756 1063 4798
πιεῖν αἰτεῖς, οὔσης γυναικὸς Σαμαρείτιδος; οὐ γὰρ συγ-
to drink ask, (1) being a woman of Samaria?   not For deal
2453   4541   611   2424 2532 2036
χρῶνται Ἰουδαῖοι Σαμαρείταις.] 10 ἀπεκρίθη Ἰησοῦς καὶ εἶπεν
with   Jews   Samaritans.)   answered Jesus and said
846 1487 1492   3588   1431 3588   2316 2532 5101 2076 3588 3004
αὐτῇ, Εἰ ᾔδεις τὴν δωρεὰν τοῦ Θεοῦ, καὶ τίς ἐστιν ὁ λέγων
to her, If you knew the gift   of God, and who is the (One) saying

---

1. When therefore the Lord knew how the Pharisees had heard that Jesus made and baptized more disciples than John,

2 (Though Jesus himself baptized not, but his disciples,)

3 He left Judaea, and departed again into Galilee.

4. And he must needs go through Samaria.

5 Then cometh he to a city of Samaria, which is called Sychar, near to the parcel of ground that Jacob gave to his son Joseph.

6 Now Jacob's well was there. Jesus therefore, being wearied with (his) journey, sat thus on the well: (and) it was about the sixth hour.

7 There cometh a woman of Samaria to draw water: Jesus saith unto her, Give me to drink.
8 (For his disciples were gone away unto the city to buy meat.)
9 Then saith the woman of Samaria unto him, How is it that thou, being a Jew, askest drink of me, which am a woman of Samaria? for the Jews have no dealings with the Samaritans.

10 Jesus answered and said unto her, If thou knewest the gift of God, and who it is that saith

Literal Translation

to you, Give Me to drink, you would have asked Him, and He would give you living water.
11 The woman said to Him, Sir, you have no vessel, and the well is deep. From where then do you have living water?
12 Are you greater than our father Jacob who gave us the well, and he and his sons and his livestock drank out of it?
13 Jesus answered and said to her, Everyone drinking of this water will thirst again;
14 But whoever may drink of the water which I will give him will not ever thirst, never! But the water which I will give to him will become a fountain of water in him, springing up into everlasting life.
15 The woman said to Him, Sir, give me this water, that I may not thirst, nor come here to draw.
16 Jesus said to her, Go, call your husband and come here.
17 And the woman answered and said, I have no husband. Jesus said to her, Well did you say, I have no husband.
18 For you have had five husbands, and now (he) whom you have is not your husband. You have spoken this truly.
19 The woman said to Him, Sir, I perceive that you are a prophet.
20 Our fathers worshiped in this mountain, and you say that in Jerusalem is the place where it is necessary to worship.
21 Jesus said to her, Woman, believe Me that an hour is coming when you will worship the Father neither in this mountain nor in Jerusalem

Greek Interlinear

4671 1325 3427 4095 4771 302 134　846　2532 1325 302 4671
σοι, Δός μοι πιεῖν, σὺ ἂν ᾔτησας αὐτόν, καὶ ἔδωκεν ἂν σοι
to you, Give Me to drink, you would have asked Him, and He would give you

5204 2198　3004 846 3588 1135 2962 3777　502 2192 2532
ὕδωρ ζῶν. 11 λέγει αὐτῷ ἡ γυνή, Κύριε, οὔτε ἄντλημα ἔχεις, καὶ
water living. says to Him the woman, Sir, no vessel You have, and

3588 5421 2076 901　4159 3767 2192 3588 5204 3588 2198 3361/4771
τὸ φρέαρ ἐστὶ βαθύ· πόθεν οὖν ἔχεις τὸ ὕδωρ τὸ ζῶν; 12 μὴ σὺ
the well is deep; from where then have you water living? Not you

3187　1488 3588 3962　2257 2384 3739 1325　2254 3588 5421
μείζων εἶ τοῦ πατρὸς ἡμῶν Ἰακώβ, ὃς ἔδωκεν ἡμῖν τὸ φρέαρ,
greater are (than) the father of us, Jacob, who gave us the well,

2532 846 1537 846　4095 2532 3588 5207 846　2532 3588 2353
καὶ αὐτὸς ἐξ αὐτοῦ ἔπιε, καὶ οἱ υἱοὶ αὐτοῦ, καὶ τὰ θρέμματα
and he out of it drank, and the sons of him, and the livestock

846　611　3588 2424 2532 2036 846 3956 3588 4095 1537
αὐτοῦ; 13 ἀπεκρίθη ὁ Ἰησοῦς καὶ εἶπεν αὐτῇ, Πᾶς ὁ πίνων ἐκ
of him? answered Jesus and said to her, Everyone drinking of

3588 5204 5127　1372 3825　3739 1161 302 4095 1537 3588
τοῦ ὕδατος τούτου, διψήσει πάλιν· 14 ὃς δ᾽ ἂν πίη ἐκ τοῦ
water this will thirst again. who But ever drinks of the

5204 3739 1473 1325 846 3756 3361 1372　1519 3588 165
ὕδατος οὗ ἐγὼ δώσω αὐτῷ, οὐ μὴ διψήσῃ εἰς τὸν αἰῶνα·
water which I will give him, not never will thirst unto the age,

235 3588 5204 3739 1325 846　1096 1722 846 4077
ἀλλὰ τὸ ὕδωρ ὃ δώσω αὐτῷ γενήσεται ἐν αὐτῷ πηγὴ
but the water which I will give him will come to be in him a fountain

5204 242 1519 2222 166　3004 4314 846 3588
ὕδατος ἁλλομένου εἰς ζωὴν αἰώνιον. 15 λέγει πρὸς αὐτὸν ἡ
of water springing up into life everlasting. says to Him the

1135 2962 1325 3427 5124 3588 5204 2443 3361 1372　3366
γυνή, Κύριε, δός μοι τοῦτο τὸ ὕδωρ, ἵνα μὴ διψῶ, μηδὲ
woman, Lord, give me this water, that not I thirst, nor

2064 1759 501　3004 846 3588 2424 5217
ἔρχωμαι ἐνθάδε ἀντλεῖν. 16 λέγει αὐτῇ ὁ Ἰησοῦς, Ὕπαγε,
come here to draw. says to her Jesus, Go,

5455 3588 435 4675 2532 2064 1759　611 3588 1135
φώνησον τὸν ἄνδρα σοῦ, καὶ ἐλθὲ ἐνθάδε. 17 ἀπεκρίθη ἡ γυνή
call the husband of you, and come here. answered the woman

2532 2036 3756 2192 435　3004 846 3588 2424 2573 2036
καὶ εἶπεν, Οὐκ ἔχω ἄνδρα. λέγει αὐτῇ ὁ Ἰησοῦς, Καλῶς εἶπας
and said, Not I have a husband. says to her Jesus, Well you say.

3754 435 3756 2192 4002 1063 435 2192 2532 3568 3739
ὅτι Ἄνδρα οὐκ ἔχω· 18 πέντε γὰρ ἄνδρας ἔσχες, καὶ νῦν ὃν
A husband not I have five For husbands you had, and now whom

2192 3756 2076 4675 435 5124 227 2046　3004 846
ἔχεις οὐκ ἔστι σου ἀνήρ· τοῦτο ἀληθὲς εἴρηκας. 19 λέγει αὐτῷ
you have not is your husband. this truly you have said. says to Him

3588 1135 2962 2334 3754 4396 1488 4771 3588 3962 2257
ἡ γυνή, Κύριε, θεωρῶ ὅτι προφήτης εἶ σύ. 20 οἱ πατέρες ἡμῶν
the woman, Lord, I perceive that a prophet are You. The fathers of us

1722 5129 3588 3735 4352 2532 5210 3004 3754 1722
ἐν τούτῳ τῷ ὄρει προσεκύνησαν· καὶ ὑμεῖς λέγετε ὅτι ἐν
in this mountain worshiped, and you say that in

2414 2076 3588 5117 3699 1163 4352　3004
Ἱεροσολύμοις ἐστὶν ὁ τόπος ὅπου δεῖ προσκυνεῖν. 21 λέγει
Jerusalem is the place where it is right to worship. says

846 3588 2424 1135 4100 3427 3754 2064 5610
αὐτῇ ὁ Ἰησοῦς, Γύναι, πίστευσόν μοι, ὅτι ἔρχεται ὥρα,
to her Jesus, Woman, believe Me that comes an hour

3753 3777 1722 3588 3735 5129 3777 1722 2414 4352
ὅτε οὔτε ἐν τῷ ὄρει τούτῳ οὔτε ἐν Ἱεροσολύμοις προσκυνή-
when not in mountain this nor in Jerusalem will you worship

King James Version

to thee, Give me to drink; thou wouldest have asked of him, and he would have given thee living water.
11 The woman saith unto him, Sir, thou hast nothing to draw with, and the well is deep: from whence then hast thou that living water?
12 Art thou greater than our father Jacob, which gave us the well, and drank thereof himself, and his children, and his cattle?
13 Jesus answered and said unto her, Whosoever drinketh of this water shall thirst again:
14 But whosoever drinketh of the water that I shall give him shall never thirst; but the water that I shall give him shall be in him a well of water springing up into everlasting life.
15 The woman saith unto him, Sir, give me this water, that I thirst not, neither come hither to draw.
16 Jesus saith unto her, Go, call thy husband, and come hither.
17 The woman answered and said, I have no husband. Jesus said unto her, Thou hast well said, I have no husband:
18 For thou hast had five husbands; and he whom thou now hast is not thy husband: in that saidst thou truly.
19 The woman saith unto him, Sir, I perceive that thou art a prophet.
20 Our fathers worshipped in this mountain; and ye say, that in Jerusalem is the place where men ought to worship.
21 Jesus saith unto her, Woman, believe me, the hour cometh, when ye shall neither in this mountain, nor yet at Jerusalem,

Literal Translation | *King James Version*

22 You worship what you do not know; we worship what we know, for salvation is of the Jews.

```
3588 3962          5210        4352      3739 3756  1492      2249
ὅτε τῷ πατρί. 22 ὑμεῖς προσκυνεῖτε ὃ οὐκ οἴδατε· ἡμεῖς
    the Father.   You     worship    what not you know;  we
4352        3739  1492   3754 3588    4991 1537 3588    2453
προσκυνοῦμεν ὃ οἴδαμεν· ὅτι ἡ σωτηρία ἐκ τῶν Ἰουδαίων
worship    what we know, since  salvation  of  the    Jews
```

22 Ye worship ye know not what: we know what we worship: for salvation is of the Jews.

23 But an hour is coming, and now is, when the true worshipers will worship the Father in spirit and in truth. For the Father also seeks such, the (ones) worshiping Him.

```
2076      235        2064    5610 2532 3568 2076 3753 3588  228
ἐστίν. 23 ἀλλ᾽ ἔρχεται ὥρα καὶ νῦν ἐστιν, ὅτε οἱ ἀληθινοὶ
  is.    But  is coming an hour, and now  is,   when the  true
4353            4352         3588  3962 1722  4151      2532
προσκυνηταὶ προσκυνήσουσι τῷ πατρὶ ἐν πνεύματι καὶ
worshipers    will worship   the Father  in  spirit   and
225       2532 1063 3588 3962      5108      2212  3588    4352
ἀληθείᾳ· καὶ γάρ ὁ πατὴρ τοιούτους ζητεῖ τοὺς προσ-
truth.   also for  the Father  such      seeks  the (ones)
```

23 But the hour cometh, and now is, when the true worshippers shall worship the Father in spirit and in truth: for the Father seeketh such to worship him.

24 God (is) spirit, and the (ones) worshiping Him must worship in spirit and truth.

```
846     4151 3588 2316 2532 3588       4352
κυνοῦντας αὐτόν. 24 Πνεῦμα ὁ Θεός· καὶ τοὺς προσκυνοῦντας
worshiping Him.      spirit  God (is), and the (ones)  worshiping
846  1722   4151 2532  225  1163   4352         3004    846
αὐτὸν, ἐν πνεύματι καὶ ἀληθείᾳ δεῖ προσκυνεῖν. 25 λέγει αὐτῷ
Him   in   spirit  and  truth  need to worship.   says  to Him
```

24 God (is) a Spirit: and they that worship him must worship (him) in spirit and in truth.

25 The woman said to Him, I know that Messiah is coming, the (One) called Christ. When that One comes, He will announce to us all things.

```
3588 1135  1492 3754  3323         2064 3588   3004        5547
ἡ γυνή, Οἶδα ὅτι Μεσσίας ἔρχεται ὁ λεγόμενος Χριστός·
The woman, I know that  Messiah  is coming, the (one) being called Christ,
3752  2064     1565     312      2254 3956     3004   846 3588
ὅταν ἔλθῃ ἐκεῖνος, ἀναγγελεῖ ἡμῖν πάντα. 26 λέγει αὐτῇ ὁ
when comes that One, He will announce to us all things.  says  to her
2424      1473 1510 3588 2980 4671
Ἰησοῦς, Ἐγώ εἰμι, ὁ λαλῶν σοι.
Jesus,   I  AM¹, the (One) speaking to you
```

25 The woman saith unto him, I know that Messias cometh, which is called Christ: when he is come, he will tell us all things.

26 Jesus said to her, I AM¹, the (One) speaking to you

26 Jesus saith unto her, I that speak unto thee am (he).

27 And on this His disciples came and marveled that He was speaking with a woman; though no one said, What do you seek? Or, Why do You speak with her?

```
2532 1909 5129     2064 3588 3101     846   2532   2296
27. Καὶ ἐπὶ τούτῳ ἦλθον οἱ μαθηταὶ αὐτοῦ, καὶ ἐθαύμασαν
And  on  this    came  the disciples of Him, and  marveled
3754 3326  1135   2980     3762   3305  2036 5101 2212
ὅτι μετὰ γυναικὸς ἐλάλει· οὐδεὶς μέντοι εἶπε, Τί ζητεῖς;
that with  a woman He was speaking; no one though  said, What seek you?
2228 5101 2980 3326   846       863      3267 3588 5201    846 3588
ἢ, Τί λαλεῖς μετ᾽ αὐτῆς; 28 ἀφῆκεν οὖν τὴν ὑδρίαν αὐτῆς ἡ
Or, Why speak You with  her?     left  Then the waterpot of her  the
1135 2532    565   1519 3588   4172 2532 3004  3588   444
γυνή, καὶ ἀπῆλθεν εἰς τὴν πόλιν, καὶ λέγει τοῖς ἀνθρώποις,
woman, and went away into  the   city,  and  says  to the   men,
```

27 And upon this came his disciples, and marvelled that he talked with the woman: yet no man said, What seekest thou? or, Why talkest thou with her?

28 Then the woman left her waterpot and went away into the city and said to the men,

28 The woman then left her waterpot, and went her way into the city, and saith to the men,

29 Come, see a Man who told me all things, whatever I did. Is this One not the Christ?

```
1205   1492    444   3739 2036 3427 3956  3745 4160    3385
29 Δεῦτε, ἴδετε ἄνθρωπον, ὃς εἶπέ μοι πάντα ὅσα ἐποίησα· μήτι
Come!  See  a Man       who told me all things whatever I did;  not
3778     2076 3588 5547            1831     3767 1537 3588 4172   2532
οὗτός ἐστιν ὁ Χριστός; 30 ἐξῆλθον οὖν ἐκ τῆς πόλεως, καὶ
this One  Is  the  Christ?    They went out, then, from the  city,   and
2064      4314  846    1722 1161 3588 3342      2065    846 3588
ἤρχοντο πρὸς αὐτόν. 31 ἐν δὲ τῷ μεταξὺ ἠρώτων αὐτὸν οἱ
came    to   Him   in  But the meantime  asked    Him the
3101      3004    4461     5315     3588 1161 2036 846      1473
μαθηταὶ, λέγοντες, Ῥαββί, φάγε. 32 ὁ δὲ εἶπεν αὐτοῖς, Ἐγὼ
disciples,  saying,   Rabbi,  eat.  He But  said  to them,   I
1035      2192 5315    3739 5210  3756  1492         3004 3767 3588
βρῶσιν ἔχω φαγεῖν ἣν ὑμεῖς οὐκ οἴδατε. 33 ἔλεγον οὖν οἱ
food    have to eat which you  not do know.  said  Then the
3101      4314  240       3387   5342    846    5315
μαθηταὶ πρὸς ἀλλήλους, Μήτις ἤνεγκεν αὐτῷ φαγεῖν;
disciples  to   one another,  No one  brought  Him  to eat?
```

29 Come, see a Man who told me all things, whatever I did. Is this One not the Christ?

29 Come, see a man, which told me all things that ever I did: is not this the Christ?

30 Therefore, they went out of the city and came to Him.

30 Then they went out of the city, and came unto him.

31 But in the meantime the disciples asked Him, saying, Master, eat?

31 In the mean while his disciples prayed him, saying, Master, eat.

32 But He said to them, I have food to eat which you do not know.

32 But he said unto them, I have meat to eat that ye know not of.

33 Then the disciples said to one another, No one brought Him (food) to eat?

33 Therefore said the disciples one to another, Hath any man brought him (ought) to eat?

34 Jesus said to them, My food is that I should do the

```
3004    846 3588 2424      1699 1033   2076  2443 4160 3588
34 λέγει αὐτοῖς ὁ Ἰησοῦς, Ἐμὸν βρῶμά ἐστιν, ἵνα ποιῶ τὸ
says  to them  Jesus,    My   food    is    that I do the
```

34 Jesus saith unto them, My meat is to do the

will of (Him) who sent Me, and that I may finish His work.

2307 3588 3992 3165 2532 5048 846 3588 2041 3756
Θέλημα τοῦ πέμψαντός με, καὶ τελειώσω αὐτοῦ τὸ ἔργον. 35 οὐχ
will of the (One) having sent Me, and I may finish of Him the work. Not

will of him that sent me, and to finish his work.

35 Do you not say, It is yet four months and the harvest comes? Behold! I say to you, Lift up your eyes and behold the fields, because they are already white to harvest.

5210 3004 3754 2089 5072 2076 2532 3588 2326 2064
ὑμεῖς λέγετε ὅτι "Ἔτι τετράμηνόν ἐστι, καὶ ὁ θερισμὸς ἔρχεται;
do you say, Yet four months, and the harvest comes?

2400 3004 5213 1869 3588 3788 5216 2532
ἰδού, λέγω ὑμῖν, Ἐπάρατε τοὺς ὀφθαλμοὺς ὑμῶν, καὶ
Behold! I say to you, Lift up the eyes of you, and

2300 3588 5561 3754 3022 1526 4314 2326 2235
θεάσασθε τὰς χώρας, ὅτι λευκαί εἰσι πρὸς θερισμὸν ἤδη.
behold the fields, because white they are to harvest already.

35 Say not ye, There are yet four months, and (then) cometh harvest? behold, I say unto you, Lift up your eyes, and look on the fields; for they are white already to harvest.

36 And the one reaping receives reward, and gathers fruit to everlasting life, so that both the (one) sowing and the (one) reaping may rejoice together.

2532 3588 2325 3408 2983 2532 4863 2590 1519 2222
36 καὶ ὁ θερίζων μισθὸν λαμβάνει, καὶ συνάγει καρπὸν εἰς ζωὴν
And the (one) reaping reward receives, and gathers fruit to life

166 2443 2532 3588 4687 3674 5463 2532 3588 2325
αἰώνιον· ἵνα καὶ ὁ σπείρων ὁμοῦ χαίρῃ καὶ ὁ θερίζων.
everlasting, that also the (one) sowing together may rejoice and he reaping.

36 And he that reapeth receiveth wages, and gathereth fruit unto life eternal: that both he that soweth and he that reapeth may rejoice together.

37 For in this the word is true, that another (is) the (one) sowing, and another the (one) reaping.

1722 1063 5129 3588 3056 2076 228 3754 243 2076 3588
37 ἐν γὰρ τούτῳ ὁ λόγος ἐστὶν ἀληθινός, ὅτι ἄλλος ἐστὶν ὁ
in For this the word is true, that another is the (one)

4687 2532 243 3588 2325 1473 649 5209 2325
σπείρων, καὶ ἄλλος ὁ θερίζων. 38 ἐγὼ ἀπέστειλα ὑμᾶς θερίζειν
sowing, and another the (one) reaping. I sent you to reap

37 And herein is that saying true, One soweth, and another reapeth.

38 I sent you to reap what you have not labored over. Others have labored, and you have entered into their labor.

3739 3756 5210 2872 243 2872 2532 5210 1519 3588
ὃ οὐχ ὑμεῖς κεκοπιάκατε· ἄλλοι κεκοπιάκασι, καὶ ὑμεῖς εἰς τὸν
what not you have labored over. Others have labored, and you into the

2873 846 1525
κόπον αὐτῶν εἰσεληλύθατε.
labor of them have entered.

38 I sent you to reap that whereon ye bestowed no labour: other men laboured, and ye are entered into their labours.

1537 1161 3588 4172 1565 4183 4100 1519 846
39. Ἐκ δὲ τῆς πόλεως ἐκείνης πολλοὶ ἐπίστευσαν εἰς αὐτὸν
out of And city that many believed into Him

39. And many of the Samaritans out of that city believed into Him, because of the word of the woman testifying, He told me all things whatever I did.

3588 4541 1223 3588 3056 3588 1135 3140
τῶν Σαμαρειτῶν διὰ τὸν λόγον τῆς γυναικὸς μαρτυρούσης,
of the Samaritans because of the word of the woman witnessing.

3754 2036 3427 3956 3745 4160 5613 3767 2064 4314 846
ὅτι Εἶπέ μοι πάντα ὅσα ἐποίησα. 40 ὡς οὖν ἦλθον πρὸς αὐτὸν
He told me all things whatever I did. as Then came to Him

39. And many of the Samaritans of that city believed on him for the saying of the woman, which testified, He told me all that ever I did.

40 Then as the Samaritans came to Him, they asked Him to remain with them. And He remained there two days.

3588 4541 2065 846 3306 3844 846 2532 3306
οἱ Σαμαρεῖται, ἠρώτων αὐτὸν μεῖναι παρ' αὐτοῖς· καὶ ἔμεινεν
the Samaritans, they asked Him to stay with them. And He stayed

1563 1417 2250 2532 4183 4119 4100 1223 3588
ἐκεῖ δύο ἡμέρας. 41 καὶ πολλῷ πλείους ἐπίστευσαν διὰ τὸν
there two days. And many more believed through the

40 So when the Samaritans were come unto him, they besought him that he would tarry with them: and he abode there two days.

41 And many more believed through His Word.

3056 846 3588 5037 1135 3004 3754 3765 1223 3588 4674
λόγον αὐτοῦ, 42 τῇ τε γυναικὶ ἔλεγον ὅτι Οὐκέτι διὰ τὴν σὴν
Word of Him to the And woman they said, No longer because of your

41 And many more believed because of his own word;

42 And they said to the woman, We no longer believe because of your speaking, for we (our)selves have heard, and we know that this One is truly the Savior of the world, the Christ.

2981 4100 846 1063 191 2532 1492 3754
λαλιὰν πιστεύομεν· αὐτοὶ γὰρ ἀκηκόαμεν, καὶ οἴδαμεν ὅτι
speaking we believe, (our)selves for we have heard, and we know that

3778 2076 230 3588 4990 3588 2889 3588 5547
οὗτός ἐστιν ἀληθῶς ὁ Σωτὴρ τοῦ κόσμου, ὁ Χριστός.
this One is truly the Savior of the world, the Christ.

42 And said unto the woman, Now we believe, not because of thy saying: for we have heard (him) ourselves, and know that this is indeed the Christ, the Saviour of the world.

43. But after the two days, He went out from there, and went away into Galilee.

3326 1161 3588 1417 2250 1831 1564 2532 565
43. Μετὰ δὲ τὰς δύο ἡμέρας ἐξῆλθεν ἐκεῖθεν, καὶ ἀπῆλθεν
after And the two days, He went out from there, and went

1519 3588 1056 846 1063 3588 2424 3140 3754
εἰς τὴν Γαλιλαίαν. 44 αὐτός γὰρ ὁ Ἰησοῦς ἐμαρτύρησεν ὅτι
into Galilee. (Him)self For Jesus testified that

43. Now after two days he departed thence, and went into Galilee.

44 For Jesus (Him)self testified that a prophet has no honor in (his) own fatherland.

4396 1722 3588 2398 3968 5092 3756 2192 3753 3767 2064
προφήτης ἐν τῇ ἰδίᾳ πατρίδι τιμὴν οὐκ ἔχει. 45 ὅτε οὖν ἦλθεν
a prophet in the own fatherland honor not has. When, then, He came

44 For Jesus himself testified, that a prophet hath no honour in his own country.

45 Therefore, when He came

45 Then when he was come

Literal Translation   *King James Version*

into Galilee, the Galilans received Him, seeing all things which He did in Jerusalem at the Feast. For they also went to the Feast.

1519 3588   1056   1209   846   3588   1057   3956
εἰς τὴν Γαλιλαίαν, ἐδέξαντο αὐτὸν οἱ Γαλιλαῖοι, πάντα
into   Galilee,   received   Him   the   Galileans, all things

3708   3739   4160   1722   2414   1722 3588 1859   2532   846
ἑωρακότες ἃ ἐποίησεν ἐν Ἱεροσολύμοις ἐν τῇ ἑορτῇ. καὶ αὐτοὶ
having seen which He did in   Jerusalem   at the feast   also they

1063   2064   1519 3588   1859
γὰρ ἦλθον εἰς τὴν ἑορτήν.
For   went   to   the   feast.

into Galilee, the Galilaeans received him, having seen all the things that he did at Jerusalem at the feast: for they also went unto the feast.

46. Then Jesus came again to Cana of Galilee where He made the water wine. And there was a certain nobleman whose son was sick in Capernaum.

2064   3767 3588 2424   3825 1519 3588 2580 3588   1056
46. Ἦλθεν οὖν ὁ Ἰησοῦς πάλιν εἰς τὴν Κανὰ τῆς Γαλιλαίας,
came Then   Jesus   again into   Cana   of Galilee,

3699   4160   3588 5204   3631 2532 2258 5100   937   3739 3588 5207
ὅπου ἐποίησε τὸ ὕδωρ οἶνον. καὶ ἦν τις βασιλικός, οὗ ὁ υἱὸς
where He made the water   wine. And was one   noble   of whom the son

46. So Jesus came again into Cana of Galilee, where he made the water wine. And there was a certain nobleman, whose son was sick at Capernaum.

47. Hearing that Jesus (was) coming from Judea into Galilee, this one went out to Him and asked Him that He would come and heal his son, for he was about to die.

770   1722   2584   3778   191   3754 2424   240 1537
ἠσθένει ἐν Καπερναούμ. 47 οὗτος ἀκούσας ὅτι Ἰησοῦς ἥκει ἐκ
was ill in Capernaum.   This one   hearing   that   Jesus comes from

3588   2449   1519 3588   1056   565   4314   846   2532
τῆς Ἰουδαίας εἰς τὴν Γαλιλαίαν, ἀπῆλθε πρὸς αὐτόν, καὶ
Judea   into   Galilee   went out to   Him,   and

2065   846   2443   2597   2532   2390   846   3588 5207
ἠρώτα αὐτὸν ἵνα καταβῇ καὶ ἰάσηται αὐτοῦ τὸν υἱόν·
asked   Him   that He would come and   heal   of him   the   son,

47. When he heard that Jesus was come out of Judaea into Galilee, he went unto him, and besought him that he would come down, and heal his son: for he was at the point of death.

48. Then Jesus said to him, Unless you see signs and wonders, you will not at all believe.

3195   1063   599   2036 3767 3588 2424   4314   846
ἤμελλε γὰρ ἀποθνῄσκειν. 48 εἶπεν οὖν ὁ Ἰησοῦς πρὸς αὐτόν,
he was for   about to die   said Then   Jesus   to   him,

48. Then said Jesus unto him, Except ye see signs and wonders, ye will not believe.

49. The nobleman said to Him, Sir, come down before my child dies.

1437 3361 4592   2532   5059   1492   3756 3361   4100   3004
Ἐὰν μὴ σημεῖα καὶ τέρατα ἴδητε, οὐ μὴ πιστεύσητε. 49 λέγει
If   not signs   and wonders you see, not at all will you believe.   says

4314   846   3588   937   2962   2597   4250   599
πρὸς αὐτὸν ὁ βασιλικός, Κύριε, κατάβηθι πρὶν ἀποθανεῖν
to   him. The   noble.   Lord, come down before   dies

49. The nobleman saith unto him, Sir, come down ere my child die.

50. Jesus said to him, Go! Your son lives. And the man believed the word which Jesus said to him, and went away.

3588   3813   3450   3004   846 3588 2424   4198   3588 5207 4675
τὸ παιδίον μου. 50 λέγει αὐτῷ ὁ Ἰησοῦς, Πορεύου· ὁ υἱός σου
the child of me.   says   to him   Jesus,   Go,   the son of you

2198   2532   4100   3588   444   3588 3056 3739 2036   846
ζῇ. καὶ ἐπίστευσεν ὁ ἄνθρωπος τῷ λόγῳ ᾧ εἶπεν αὐτῷ
lives. And   believed   the   man   the   word which said to him

50. Jesus saith unto him, Go thy way; thy son liveth. And the man believed the word that Jesus had spoken unto him, and he went his way.

51. But already, as he was going down, his slaves met him and reported, saying, Your child lives.

2424   2532   4198   2235 1161 846   2597   3588
Ἰησοῦς, καὶ ἐπορεύετο. 51 ἤδη δὲ αὐτοῦ καταβαίνοντος, οἱ
Jesus,   and went away.   already And (as) he was going down, the

1401   846   528   846   2532   518   3004
δοῦλοι αὐτοῦ ἀπήντησαν αὐτῷ, καὶ ἀπήγγειλαν λέγοντες
slaves   of him   met   him,   and   reported,   saying,

51. And as he was now going down, his servants met him, and told (him), saying, Thy son liveth.

52. He then asked from them the hour in which he had gotten better. And they said to him, Yesterday, (at the) seventh hour, the fever left him.

3754 3588 3816 4675 2198   4441   3767 3844   846   3588   5610 1722
ὅτι Ὁ παῖς σου ζῇ. 52 ἐπύθετο οὖν παρ' αὐτῶν τὴν ὥραν ἐν
The child of you lives   he asked Then from   them   the   hour   in

3739   2866   2192 2532 2036   846   3754   5504   5610   1442
ᾗ κομψότερον ἔσχε· καὶ εἶπον αὐτῷ ὅτι Χθὲς ὥραν ἑβδόμην
which become better he had And they said to him,   Yesterday (at) hour seventh

52. Then enquired he of them the hour when he began to amend. And they said unto him, Yesterday at the seventh hour the fever left him.

53. Then the father knew that (it was) at that hour in which Jesus said to him, Your son lives. And he himself, and his whole house, believed.

863   846 3588   4446   1097 3767 3588 3962 3754 1722 1565   3588
ἀφῆκεν αὐτὸν ὁ πυρετός. 53 ἔγνω οὖν ὁ πατὴρ ὅτι ἐν ἐκείνῃ τῇ
left   him the fever.   knew Then the father that in   that

5610   1722 3739 2036   846 3588   2424   3754 3588 5207 4675 2198 2532
ὥρᾳ, ἐν ᾗ εἶπεν αὐτῷ ὁ Ἰησοῦς ὅτι Ὁ υἱός σου ζῇ· καὶ
hour, in which said to him   Jesus,   The son of you lives, and

53. So the father knew that (it was) at the same hour, in the which Jesus said unto him, Thy son liveth: and himself believed, and his whole house.

54. Again, this second sign Jesus did, coming from Judea.

4100   846   2532 3588 3614   846   3650   5124   3825
ἐπίστευσεν αὐτὸς καὶ ἡ οἰκία αὐτοῦ ὅλη. 54 τοῦτο πάλιν
he believed,   himself and the house of him whole.   This again

1208   4592   4160   3588 2424   2064 1537 3588   2449
δεύτερον σημεῖον ἐποίησεν ὁ Ἰησοῦς ἐλθὼν ἐκ τῆς Ἰουδαίας
a second   sign   did   Jesus,   coming from   Judea

54. This (is) again the second miracle (that) Jesus did, when he was come out of Judaea

Acrostic Index

The following is the full chapter, in English and in Greek of John: Chapter 21, Verse 17, where acrostic 7 begins, is clearly marked.

1. After these things Jesus revealed Himself again to the disciples at the Sea of Tiberias. And He revealed (Himself) in this way:

```
3326    5023    5319         1438    3825 3588 2424  3588
1 Μετὰ  ταῦτα   ἐφανέρωσεν   ἑαυτὸν  πάλιν  ὁ  Ἰησοῦς τοῖς
  After  these things revealed Himself again    Jesus to the

3101       1909 3588  2281      3588  5085       5319      1161
μαθηταῖς   ἐπὶ τῆς θαλάσσης   τῆς Τιβεριάδος·  ἐφανέρωσε   δὲ
disciples  at  the   Sea      of  Tiberias.    He revealed And
```

1. After these things Jesus shewed himself again to the disciples at the sea of Tiberias; and on this wise shewed he (himself).

2 Simon Peter, and Thomas, being called Twin, and Nathanael from Cana of Galilee, and the (sons) of Zebedee, and two others of His disciples were together

```
3779    2258  3674  4613    4074    2532 2381  3588  3004
οὕτως. 2 ἦσαν ὁμοῦ Σίμων  Πέτρος, καὶ Θωμᾶς ὁ λεγόμενος
in this way: Were together Simon  Peter,  and Thomas being called

1324     2532 3482      3588 575 2580  3588  1056      2532 3588
Δίδυμος, καὶ Ναθαναὴλ ὁ  ἀπὸ Κανᾶ τῆς Γαλιλαίας, καὶ οἱ
Twin,    and Nathanael the (one) from Cana of Galilee, and those

3588  2199       2532 243   1537 3588 3101     846    1417
τοῦ Ζεβεδαίου,  καὶ ἄλλοι ἐκ  τῶν  μαθητῶν αὐτοῦ  δύο.
of Zebedee,     and others from the disciples of Him two.
```

2 There were together Simon Peter, and Thomas called Didymus, and Nathanael of Cana in Galilee, and the (sons) of Zebedee, and two other of his disciples.

3 Simon Peter said to them, I am going out to fish. They said to him, We also are coming with you. They went and went up into the boat at once. And in that night, they caught nothing.

```
3004    846    4613    4074    5217          232      3004
3 λέγει αὐτοῖς Σίμων  Πέτρος, Ὑπάγω ἁλιεύειν. λέγουσιν
  says  to them Simon  Peter,  I am going to fish.  They say

846    2064       2532 2249 4862 4671  1831    2532 305
αὐτῷ, Ἐρχόμεθα  καὶ ἡμεῖς σὺν σοί. ἐξῆλθον καὶ ἀνέβησαν
to him, are coming also We   with you. They went and went up

1519 3588 4143   2117  2532 1722 1565  3588 3571  4084     3762
εἰς τὸ πλοῖον εὐθύς, καὶ ἐν ἐκείνῃ τῇ νυκτὶ ἐπίασαν οὐδέν.
into the boat  at once And in that    night, they caught nothing.
```

3 Simon Peter saith unto them, I go a fishing. They say unto him, We also go with thee. They went forth, and entered into a ship immediately; and that night they caught nothing.

4 And it now becoming early morning, Jesus stood on the shore. However, the disciples did not know that it was Jesus.

```
4405     1161 2235  1096        2476 3588 2424  1519 3588 123
4 πρωΐας δὲ ἤδη γενομένης ἔστη ὁ Ἰησοῦς εἰς τὸν αἰγιαλόν·
  early morn And now (it) becoming stood Jesus onto the shore.

3756 3305   1492       3588 3101    3754 2424  2076  3004 3767
οὐ μέντοι ᾔδεισαν οἱ μαθηταὶ ὅτι Ἰησοῦς ἐστι. 5 λέγει οὖν
not However knew the disciples that Jesus it is.    says Then
```

4 But when the morning was now come, Jesus stood on the shore: but the disciples knew not that it was Jesus.

5 Then Jesus said to them, Children, do you not have anything for eating? They answered Him, No.

```
846    3588 2424   3813   3361 5100 4371       2192   611
αὐτοῖς ὁ Ἰησοῦς, Παιδία, μή τι προσφάγιον ἔχετε; ἀπεκρί-
to them  Jesus,  Children, not anything for eating have you? They
```

5 Then Jesus saith unto them, Children, have ye any meat? They answered him, No.

6 And He said to them, Cast the net to the right parts of the boat and you will find.

```
846     3756 3588 1161 2036   846     906    1519 3588 1188
θησαν αὐτῷ, Οὔ. 6 ὁ δὲ εἶπεν αὐτοῖς, Βάλετε εἰς τὰ δεξιὰ
answered to Him, No. He And said to them, Cast to the right

3313 3588 4143   3588 1350   2532 2147       906    3767 2532
μέρη τοῦ πλοίου τὸ δίκτυον, καὶ εὑρήσετε. ἔβαλον οὖν, καὶ
parts of the boat the net,   and you will find. they cast Then, and
```

6 And he said unto them, Cast the net on the right side of the ship, and ye shall find. They cast therefore, and now they were not able to draw it for the multitude of fishes.

7 Then they cast, and they no longer had (the) strength to draw it, from the multitude of the fish. Then the disciple whom Jesus loved said to Peter, It is the Lord. Then hearing that it is the Lord, Simon Peter having girded on (his) coat, for he was naked, and threw himself into the sea.

```
3765    846   1670      2480     575 3588 4128      3588
οὐκέτι αὐτὸ ἑλκύσαι ἴσχυσαν ἀπὸ τοῦ πλήθους τῶν
no longer it to draw they had strength, from the multitude of the

2486    3004 3767 3588 3101   1565  3739  25  3588 2424
ἰχθύων. 7 λέγει οὖν ὁ μαθητὴς ἐκεῖνος ὃν ἠγάπα ὁ Ἰησοῦς
fish     says Then  disciple that whom loved Jesus

3588 4074   3588 2962   2076  4613 3767 4074  191 3754 3588
τῷ Πέτρῳ, Ὁ Κύριός ἐστι. Σίμων οὖν Πέτρος, ἀκούσας ὅτι ὁ
to Peter, the Lord It is. Simon Then Peter, hearing that the

2962   2076  3588 1903      1241     2258 1063 1131   2532
Κύριός ἐστι, τὸν ἐπενδύτην διεζώσατο ἦν γὰρ γυμνός), καὶ
Lord it is. the coat having girded on, he was for naked, and

906     1438 1519 3588  2281     3588 1161 243  3101   3588
ἔβαλεν ἑαυτὸν εἰς τὴν θάλασσαν· 8 οἱ δὲ ἄλλοι μαθηταὶ τῷ
threw  himself into the sea.     the And other disciples in the
```

7 Therefore that disciple whom Jesus loved saith unto Peter, It is the Lord. Now when Simon Peter heard that it was the Lord, he girt (his) fisher's coat (unto him), (for he was naked,) and did cast himself into the sea.

8 And the other disciples in the

John 21:9

Literal Translation

in the little boat came. for they were not far from the land, but from about two hundred cubits, dragging the net of the fish.

9 Then when they went up onto the land, they saw a fire of coals lying, and a fish having been laid on (it), and bread. 10 Jesus said to them, Bring from the little fish which you caught now.

11 Simon Peter went up, and dragged the net onto the land, full of big fish, a hundred and fifty three. And (though) being so many, the net was not torn. 12 Jesus said to them, Come, break fast. And no one of the disciples dared to ask Him, Who are You? knowing that it is the Lord.

13 Then Jesus comes and takes the bread, and gives to them, and in the same way the little fish. 14 This now (is) the three times (that) Jesus was revealed to His disciples, (He) having been raised from (the) dead.

15. Then when they broke fast, Jesus said to Simon Peter, Simon, (son) of Jonah, do you love Me more (than) these? He said to Him, Yes, Lord, You know that I love You. He said to him, Feed My lambs! 16 Again He says to him secondly, Simon, (son) of Jonah, do you love Me? He says to Him, Yes, Lord, You know that I love You. He says to him, Shepherd My sheep! 17 Thirdly, He said to him, Simon (son) of Jonah, do you love Me? Peter was grieved that He said to him a third (time). Do you love Me? And he said to him, Lord, You perceive all things, You know that

Interlinear (Greek)

4142 2064 3756 1063 2258 3112 575 3588 1093 235
πλοιαρίω ἦλθον [οὐ γὰρ ἦσαν μακρὰν ἀπὸ τῆς γῆς, ἀλλ'
little boat came, not for they were far from the land, but

5613 575 4083 1250 4951 3588 1350 3588
ὡς ἀπὸ πηχῶν διακοσίων], σύροντες τὸ δίκτυον τῶν
about from cubits two hundred, dragging the net of the

2486 5613 3767 576 1519 3588 1093 991 439
ἰχθύων. 9 ὡς οὖν ἀπέβησαν εἰς τὴν γῆν, βλέπουσιν ἀνθρακιὰν
fish. when Then they went up onto the land, they saw a fire of coals

2749 2532 3795 1945 2532 740 3004 846
κειμένην καὶ ὀψάριον ἐπικείμενον, καὶ ἄρτον. 10 λέγει αὐτοῖς
lying, and a fish having been laid on, and bread. says to them

3588 2424 5342 575 3588 3795 3739 4084 3568
ὁ Ἰησοῦς, Ἐνέγκατε ἀπὸ τῶν ὀψαρίων ὧν ἐπιάσατε νῦν.
Jesus, Bring from the little fish which you caught now.

305 4613 4074 2532 1670 3588 1350 1909 3588 1093
11 ἀνέβη Σίμων Πέτρος, καὶ εἵλκυσε τὸ δίκτυον ἐπὶ τῆς γῆς,
went up Simon Peter, and dragged the net onto the land,

3324 2486 3173 1540 4004 2532
μεστὸν ἰχθύων μεγάλων· ἑκατὸν πεντηκοντατριῶν· καὶ
full fish of great, a hundred fifty three. And

5118 5607 3756 4977 3588 1350 3004 846 3588
τοσούτων ὄντων, οὐκ ἐσχίσθη τὸ δίκτυον. 12 λέγει αὐτοῖς ὁ
so many being, not was torn the net. says to them

2424 1205 709 3762 1161 5111 3588 3101
Ἰησοῦς, Δεῦτε ἀριστήσατε. οὐδεὶς δὲ ἐτόλμα τῶν μαθητῶν
Jesus, Come, break fast. no one And dared of the disciples

1833 846 4771 5101 1488 1492 3754 3588 2962 2076
ἐξετάσαι αὐτόν, Σὺ τίς εἶ; εἰδότες ὅτι ὁ Κύριός ἐστιν.
to question Him, You Who are? Knowing that the Lord it is.

2064 3767 2424 2532 2983 3588 740 2532 1325
13 ἔρχεται οὖν Ἰησοῦς, καὶ λαμβάνει τὸν ἄρτον, καὶ δίδωσιν
comes Then Jesus, and takes the bread, and gives

846 2532 3588 3795 3668 5124 2235 5154 5319
αὐτοῖς, καὶ τὸ ὀψάριον ὁμοίως. 14 τοῦτο ἤδη τρίτον ἐφανερώθη
to them, and the little fish likewise. This now thrice was revealed

3588 2424 3588 3101 846 1453 1537 3498
ὁ Ἰησοῦς τοῖς μαθηταῖς αὐτοῦ, ἐγερθεὶς ἐκ νεκρῶν.
Jesus to the disciples of Him, having been raised from (the) dead.

3753 3767 709 3004 3588 4613 4074 3588 2424
15 Ὅτε οὖν ἠρίστησαν, λέγει τῷ Σίμωνι Πέτρῳ ὁ Ἰησοῦς,
when Then they broke fast, says to Simon Peter Jesus,

4613 2495 25 3165 4119 5130 3004 846 3483
Σίμων Ἰωνᾶ, ἀγαπᾷς με πλεῖον τούτων; λέγει αὐτῷ, Ναί,
Simon (son) of Jonah, do you love Me more (than) these? He says to Him, Yes,

2962 4771 1492 3754 5368 4571 3004 846 1006 3588 721 3450
Κύριε· σὺ οἶδας ὅτι φιλῶ σε. λέγει αὐτῷ, Βόσκε τὰ ἀρνία μου.
Lord. You know that I love You. He says to him, Feed the lambs of Me.

3004 846 3825 1208 4613 2495 25 3165 3004
16 λέγει αὐτῷ πάλιν δεύτερον, Σίμων Ἰωνᾶ, ἀγαπᾷς με; λέγει
He says to him again, secondly, Simon of Jonah, do you love Me? He says

846 3483 2962 4771 1492 3754 5368 4571 3004 846 4165
αὐτῷ, Ναί Κύριε· σὺ οἶδας ὅτι φιλῶ σε. λέγει αὐτῷ, Ποίμαινε
to Him, Yes. Lord, You know that I love You. He says to him, Shepherd

3588 4263 3450 3004 846 3588 5154 4613 2495 5368
τὰ πρόβατά μου. 17 λέγει αὐτῷ τὸ τρίτον, Σίμων Ἰωνᾶ, φιλεῖς
the sheep of Me He says to him thirdly, Simon of Jonah, do you love

3165 3076 3588 4074 3754 2036 846 3588 5154 5368 3165
με; ἐλυπήθη ὁ Πέτρος ὅτι εἶπεν αὐτῷ τὸ τρίτον, φιλεῖς με;
Me? was grieved Peter because He said to him thirdly. Do you love Me?

2532 2036 846 2962 4771 3956 1492 4771 1097 3754
καὶ εἶπεν αὐτῷ, Κύριε, σὺ πάντα οἶδας, σὺ γινώσκεις ὅτι
And he said to Him, Lord, You all things perceive, You know that

King James Version

came in a little ship, (for they were not far from land, but as it were two hundred cubits,) dragging the net with fishes.

9 As soon then as they were come to land, they saw a fire of coals there, and fish laid thereon, and bread. 10 Jesus saith unto them, Bring of the fish which ye have now caught.

11 Simon Peter went up, and drew the net to land full of great fishes, an hundred and fifty and three: and for all there were so many, yet was not the net broken. 12 Jesus saith unto them, Come (and) dine. And none of the disciples durst ask him, Who art thou? knowing that it was the Lord.

13 Jesus then cometh, and taketh bread, and giveth them, and fish likewise. 14 This is now the third time that Jesus shewed himself to his disciples, after that he was risen from the dead.

15. So when they had dined, Jesus saith to Simon Peter, Simon, (son) of Jonas, lovest thou me more than these? He saith unto him, Yea, Lord; thou knowest that I love thee. He saith unto him, Feed my lambs. 16 He saith to him again the second time, Simon, (son) of Jonas, lovest thou me? He saith unto him, Yea, Lord; thou knowest that I love thee. He saith unto him, Feed my sheep. 17 He saith unto him the third time, Simon, (son) of Jonas, lovest thou me? Peter was grieved because he said unto him the third time, Lovest thou me? And he said unto him, Lord, thou knowest all things; thou knowest that

Literal Translation	John 21:18	King James Version

Literal Translation

I love You! Jesus says to him. Feed My sheep!

18 Truly, truly, I say to you, when you were younger, you girded yourself, and you walked where you desired. But when you grow old, you will stretch out your hands, and another will gird you, and will carry (you) where you do not desire.

19 But He said this, signifying by what death he will glorify God. And having said this, He told him, Follow Me.

20 But turning, Peter sees the disciple whom Jesus loved following, who also leaned on His breast at the Supper, and said, Lord, who is the (one) betraying You?

21 Seeing this one, Peter said to Jesus, Lord, and what (of) this one?

22 Jesus says to him, If I desire him to remain until I come, what (is that) to you? You follow Me.

23 Therefore, the word went out to the brothers that that disciple does not die. Yet Jesus did not say to him that he does not die, but, If I desire him to remain until I come, what (is that) to you?

24 This is the disciple witnessing about these things, writing these things, and we know that his witness is true.

25 And many are the things whatever Jesus did, which if they were written singly, I suppose the world itself (could) not contain the scrolls having been written. Amen.

Greek with Strong's numbers

5368 4571 3004 846 3588 2424 1006 3588 4263 3450 281
λέγει αὐτῷ ὁ Ἰησοῦς, Βόσκε τὰ πρόβατά μου. 18 ἀμὴν
I love You, says to him Jesus, Feed the sheep of Me. Truly,

281 3004 4671 3753 2258 3501 2224 4572 2532
ἀμὴν λέγω σοι, ὅτε ἧς νεώτερος, ἐζώννυες σεαυτόν, καὶ
Truly, I say to you, when you were younger, you girded yourself, and

4043 3699 2309 3752 1161 1095 1614 1588
περιεπάτεις ὅπου ἤθελες, ὅταν δὲ γηράσῃς, ἐκτενεῖς τὰς
you walked where you desired, when but you grow old, you will stretch the

5495 4675 2532 243 4571 2224 2532 5342 3699 3756 2309
χεῖράς σου, καὶ ἄλλος σε ζώσει καὶ οἴσει ὅπου οὐ θέλεις.
hands of you, and another you will gird, and will carry where not you desire.

5124 1161 2036 4591 4169 2288 1392 3588 2316
19 τοῦτο δὲ εἶπε, σημαίνων ποίῳ θανάτῳ δοξάσει τὸν Θεόν.
this But He said, signifying by what death he will glorify God.

2532 5124 2036 3004 846 190 3427 1994
καὶ τοῦτο εἰπὼν λέγει αὐτῷ, Ἀκολούθει μοι. 20 Ἐπιστραφεὶς
And this having said He says to him, Follow Me. turning

1161 3588 4074 991 3588 3101 3739 25 3588 2424 190
δὲ ὁ Πέτρος βλέπει τὸν μαθητὴν ὃν ἠγάπα ὁ Ἰησοῦς ἀκολου-
And Peter sees the disciple whom loved Jesus following,

3739 2532 377 1722 3588 1173 1909 3588 4738 846
θοῦντα, ὃς καὶ ἀνέπεσεν ἐν τῷ δείπνῳ ἐπὶ τὸ στῆθος αὐτοῦ
who also leaned at the Supper on the breast of Him,

2532 2036 2962 5101 2076 3588 3860 4571 5126 1492 3588
καὶ εἶπε, Κύριε, τίς ἐστιν ὁ παραδιδούς σε; 21 τοῦτον ἰδὼν ὁ
and said, Lord, who is the (one) betraying You? this one seeing

4074 3004 3588 2424 2962 3778 1161 5101 3004 846 3588
Πέτρος λέγει τῷ Ἰησοῦ, Κύριε, οὗτος δὲ τί; 22 λέγει αὐτῷ ὁ
Peter says to Jesus, Lord, this one and what? says to him

2424 1437 846 2309 3306 2193 2064 5101 4314 4571
Ἰησοῦς, Ἐὰν αὐτὸν θέλω μένειν ἕως ἔρχομαι, τί πρός σε;
Jesus, If him I desire to remain until I come, what to you?

4771 190 3427 1831 3767 3588 3056 3778 1519 3588 80
σύ ἀκολούθει μοι. 23 ἐξῆλθεν οὖν ὁ λόγος οὗτος εἰς τοὺς ἀδελ-
You follow Me. went out Then word this to the brothers,

3754 3588 3101 1565 3756 599 2532 3756 2036
φούς, ὅτι ὁ μαθητὴς ἐκεῖνος οὐκ ἀποθνῄσκει· καὶ οὐκ εἶπεν
that the disciple that not does die. Yet not said

846 3588 2424 3754 3756 599 235 1437 846 2309
αὐτῷ ὁ Ἰησοῦς, ὅτι οὐκ ἀποθνῄσκει· ἀλλ᾽, Ἐὰν αὐτὸν θέλω
to him Jesus, that not he does die, but, If him I desire

3306 2193 2064 5101 4314 4571
μένειν ἕως ἔρχομαι, τί πρός σε;
to remain until I come, what to you?

3778 2076 3588 3101 3588 3140 4012 5130 2532
24 Οὗτός ἐστιν ὁ μαθητὴς ὁ μαρτυρῶν περὶ τούτων, καὶ
This is the disciple witnessing concerning these things, and

1125 5023 2532 1492 3754 227 2076 3588 3141
γράψας ταῦτα· καὶ οἴδαμεν ὅτι ἀληθής ἐστιν ἡ μαρτυρία
writing these things, and we know that true is the witness

846
αὐτοῦ.
of him

2076 1161 2532 243 4183 3745 4160 3588 2424 3748
25 Ἔστι δὲ καὶ ἄλλα πολλὰ ὅσα ἐποίησεν ὁ Ἰησοῦς, ἅτινα
are And also the things many whatever did Jesus, which

1437 1125 2596 1520 3761 846 3633 3588 2889 5562
ἐὰν γράφηται καθ᾽ ἕν, οὐδὲ αὐτὸν οἶμαι τὸν κόσμον χωρῆσαι
if they were written singly, not itself I suppose the world to contain

3588 1125 975 281
τὰ γραφόμενα βιβλία. Ἀμήν.
those having been written scrolls. Amen

King James Version

I love thee. Jesus saith unto him, Feed my sheep.

18 Verily, verily, I say unto thee, When thou wast young, thou girdedst thyself, and walkedst whither thou wouldest: but when thou shalt be old, thou shalt stretch forth thy hands, and another shall gird thee, and carry (thee) whither thou wouldest not.

19 This spake he, signifying by what death he should glorify God. And when he had spoken this, he saith unto him, Follow me.

20 Then Peter, turning about, seeth the disciple whom Jesus loved following; which also leaned on his breast at supper, and said, Lord, which is he that betrayeth thee?

21 Peter seeing him saith to Jesus, Lord, and what (shall) this man (do)?

22 Jesus saith unto him, If I will that he tarry till I come, what (is that) to thee? follow thou me.

23 Then went this saying abroad among the brethren, that that disciple should not die: yet Jesus said not unto him, He shall not die; but, If I will that he tarry till I come, what (is that) to thee?

24 This is the disciple which testifieth of these things, and wrote these things: and we know that his testimony is true.

25 And there are also many other things which Jesus did, the which, if they should be written every one, I suppose that even the world itself could not contain the books that should be written. Amen.

Acrostic Index

The following is the full chapter, in English and in Greek of Romans: Chapter 8, Verse 34, where acrostic 8 begins, is clearly marked.

3762   686   3568   2631   3588 1722 5547   2424 3361
1. Οὐδὲν   ἄρα νῦν   κατάκριμα τοῖς ἐν Χριστῷ Ἰησοῦ, μὴ
   no   Therefore now condemnation to those in   Christ   Jesus, not

2596   4561   4043   235 2596   4151   3588 1063 3551
κατὰ σάρκα περιπατοῦσιν, ἀλλὰ κατὰ πνεῦμα. 2 ὁ γὰρ νόμος
according to flesh walking,   but according to Spirit. the For law of the

3588   4151   3588 2222 1722 5547   2424   1659   3165 575
τοῦ πνεύματος τῆς ζωῆς ἐν Χριστῷ Ἰησοῦ ἠλευθέρωσέ με ἀπὸ
Spirit   of life in Christ   Jesus   set free   me from

3588   3551 3588   266   2532 3588   2288   3588 1063 102
τοῦ νόμου τῆς ἁμαρτίας καὶ τοῦ θανάτου. 3 τὸ γὰρ ἀδύνατον
the law   of sin   and of death.   the For powerless

3588   3551   1722 3739 770   1223 3588 4561   3588 2316   3588
τοῦ νόμου, ἐν ᾧ, ἠσθένει διὰ τῆς σαρκός, ὁ Θεὸς τὸν
law,   in which it was weak through the flesh,   God   the

1438   5207   3992   1722   3667   4561   266   2532 4012
ἑαυτοῦ υἱὸν πέμψας ἐν ὁμοιώματι σαρκὸς ἁμαρτίας καὶ περὶ
of Himself Son sending in likeness   of flesh of sin and concerning

266   2632   3588   266   1722 3588 4561   2443 3588 1345
ἁμαρτίας κατέκρινε τὴν ἁμαρτίαν ἐν τῇ σαρκί 4 ἵνα τὸ δικαίω-
sin   condemned   sin   in the flesh;   that the righteous-

3588   3551   4137   1722 1254 3588 3361 2596 4561   4043
μα τοῦ νόμου πληρωθῇ ἐν ἡμῖν, τοῖς μὴ κατὰ σάρκα περιπατοῦ-
ness of the law may be fulfilled in us, the (ones) not according to flesh walking.

235 2596   4151   3588 1063 2596   4561   5607 3588/3588
σιν, ἀλλὰ κατὰ πνεῦμα. 5 οἱ γὰρ κατὰ σάρκα ὄντες τὰ τῆς
but according to Spirit. the (ones) For according to flesh being the things

4561   5426   3588 1161 2596   4151   3588 3588   4151   3588
σαρκὸς φρονοῦσιν· οἱ δὲ κατὰ πνεῦμα τὰ τοῦ πνεύματος. 6 τὸ
of flesh mind. the (ones) but according to Spirit the things of the Spirit   the

1063   5427   3588   4561   2288   3588 1161 5427   3588   4151
γὰρ φρόνημα τῆς σαρκὸς θάνατος· τὸ δὲ φρόνημα τοῦ πνεύμα-
For   mind   of the flesh (is) death; the but mind   of the Spirit

2222 2532 1515   1360 3588 5427   3588 4561   2189 1519
τος ζωὴ καὶ εἰρήνη· 7 διότι τὸ φρόνημα τῆς σαρκὸς ἔχθρα εἰς
(is) life and peace,   because the mind of the flesh (is) hostile toward

2316   3588 1063 3551   3588 2316   3756   5293   3761 1063
Θεόν, τῷ γὰρ νόμῳ τοῦ Θεοῦ οὐχ ὑποτάσσεται, οὐδὲ γὰρ
God, to the For law of God not it is being subjected, neither for

1410   3588 1161 1722 4561 5607   2316   700   3756 1410
δύναται· 8 οἱ δὲ ἐν σαρκὶ ὄντες Θεῷ ἀρέσαι οὐ δύνανται.
can it (be); the (ones) but in flesh being God to please not is able.

5210 1161 3756 2075 1722 4561   235 1722 4151   1512 4151
9 ὑμεῖς δὲ οὐκ ἐστὲ ἐν σαρκὶ, ἀλλ᾽ ἐν πνεύματι, εἴπερ Πνεῦμα
But not are in flesh, but in Spirit, if indeed (the) Spirit

2316   3611   1722 5213 1487 1161 5100 4151   5547   3756 2192   3778
Θεοῦ οἰκεῖ ἐν ὑμῖν. εἰ δέ τις Πνεῦμα Χριστοῦ οὐκ ἔχει, οὗτος
of God dwells in you. if But anyone (the) Spirit of Christ not has, this one

3756   2076   846   1487 1161 5547   1722 5213 3588 3303 4983   3498
οὐκ ἔστιν αὐτοῦ. 10 εἰ δὲ Χριστὸς ἐν ὑμῖν, τὸ μὲν σῶμα νεκρὸν
not is of Him   if But Christ (is) in you, the indeed body (is) dead

---

1. (There is) therefore now no condemnation to the (ones) in Christ Jesus, who do not walk according to flesh, but according to Spirit.
2 For the law of the Spirit of life in Christ Jesus set me free from the law of sin and of death.

3 For the law (being) powerless, in that it was weak through the flesh, God sending His own Son in (the) likeness of sinful flesh, and concerning sin condemned sin in the flesh.

4 So that the righteousness of the law might be fulfilled in us, the (ones) not walking according to flesh, but according to Spirit.

5 For the ones being according to flesh mind the things of the flesh, but the ones according to Spirit (mind) the things of the Spirit.
6 For the mind of the flesh (is) death, but the mind of the Spirit (is) life and peace;
7 because the mind of the flesh (is) hostile towards God; for it is not being subjected to the law of God, for neither can (it be).
8 And the (ones) being in (the) flesh are not able to please God
9 But you are not in flesh, but in Spirit, if indeed (the) Spirit of God dwells in you. But if anyone has not (the) Spirit of Christ, this one is not His.
10 But if Christ (is) in you, the body indeed (is) dead

---

1. (There is) therefore now no condemnation to them which are in Christ Jesus, who walk not after the flesh, but after the Spirit.
2 For the law of the Spirit of life in Christ Jesus hath made me free from the law of sin and death.
3 For what the law could not do, in that it was weak through the flesh, God sending his own Son in the likeness of sinful flesh, and for sin, condemned sin in the flesh:

4 That the righteousness of the law might be fulfilled in us, who walk not after the flesh, but after the Spirit.

5 For they that are after the flesh do mind the things of the flesh; but they that are after the Spirit the things of the Spirit.

6 For to be carnally minded (is) death; but to be spiritually minded (is) life and peace.
7 Because the carnal mind (is) enmity against God: for it is not subject to the law of God, neither indeed can be.
8 So then they that are in the flesh cannot please God.
9 But ye are not in the flesh, but in the Spirit, if so be that the Spirit of God dwell in you. Now if any man have not the Spirit of Christ, he is none of his.
10 And if Christ (be) in you, the body (is) dead

because of sin, but the
Spirit (is) life because of
righteousness.
11 But if the Spirit of the
(One) having raised Je-
sus from (the) dead
dwells in you, the (One)
having raised the Christ
from (the) dead will
also make your mortal
bodies live through the
indwelling of His Spirit
in you.

```
1223    205      3588 1161 4151    2222 1223    1343           1487/1161/3588
δι' ἁμαρτίαν, τὸ δὲ πνεῦμα ζωὴ διὰ δικαιοσύνην. 11 εἰ δὲ τὸ
because of sin,    the but Spirit (is) life because of righteousness    if  But the

4151       3588      1453          2424 1537    3498      3611 1722 5213 3588
Πνεῦμα τοῦ ἐγείραντος Ἰησοῦν ἐκ νεκρῶν οἰκεῖ ἐν ὑμῖν, ὁ
Spirit of the (One) having raised   Jesus  from (the) dead  dwells  in  you,  He

1453     3588      5547   1537 3498        2227        2532 3588 2349
ἐγείρας τὸν Χριστὸν ἐκ νεκρῶν ζωοποιήσει καὶ τὰ θνητὰ
having raised   Christ   from (the) dead   will make live   also  the  mortal

4983      5216  1223 3588        1774      846       4151     1722
σώματα ὑμῶν. διὰ τοῦ ἐνοικοῦντος αὐτοῦ Πνεύματος ἐν
body     of you, through the    indwelling     of Him   Spirit    in

5213
ὑμῖν.
you.
```

because of sin; but the
Spirit (is) life because of
righteousness.
11 But if the Spirit of
him that raised up Jesus
from the dead dwell in
you, he that raised up
Christ from the dead
shall also quicken your
mortal bodies by his
Spirit that dwelleth in
you.

12 So, then, brothers,
we are debtors, not to
the flesh, to live according to flesh;
13 for if you live ac-
cording to flesh, you're
going to die, but if by
(the) Spirit you put to
death the practices of
the body, you will live.

```
686 3767     80        3781      2070 3756 3588 4561 3588 2596
12 Ἄρα οὖν, ἀδελφοί, ὀφειλέται ἐσμέν, οὐ τῇ σαρκὶ, τοῦ κατὰ
So then,  brothers,   debtors     we are, not to the flesh,  according to

4561    2198    1487 1063 2596    4561    2198     3195        599
σάρκα ζῆν· 13 εἰ γὰρ κατὰ σάρκα ζῆτε μέλλετε ἀποθνήσκειν,
flesh   to live,   if for according to flesh you live, you are going to die,

1487 1161 4151    3588    4234       3588    4983        2289       2198
εἰ δὲ πνεύματι τὰς πράξεις τοῦ σώματος θανατοῦτε, ζήσεσθε.
if but by (the) Spirit the practices of the  body    you put to death, you will live.
```

12 Therefore, brethren,
we are debtors, not to
the flesh, to live after the
flesh.
13 For if ye live after the
flesh, ye shall die: but if
ye through the Spirit do
mortify the deeds of the
body, ye shall live.

14 For as many as are
led by (the) Spirit of
God, these are sons of
God.
15 For you did not re-
ceive a spirit of slavery
again to fear, but you received a Spirit of adop-
tion, by which we cry,
Abba! Father!

```
3745 1063    4151    2316   71      3778     1520 5207    2316
14 ὅσοι γὰρ Πνεύματι Θεοῦ ἄγονται, οὗτοι εἰσιν υἱοί Θεοῦ.
as many as For  by Spirit  of God are led,  these   are   sons of God

3756 1063    2983    4151      1397       3825 1519 5401    235
15 οὐ γὰρ ἐλάβετε πνεῦμα δουλείας πάλιν εἰς φόβον, ἀλλ'
not For  you received  a spirit  of slavery   again  to  fear,   but

2983    4151      5206    1722 3739 2896    5      3588 3962
ἐλάβετε πνεῦμα υἱοθεσίας, ἐν ᾧ κράζομεν, Ἀββᾶ ὁ πατήρ·
you received  a spirit   of adoption,  by which we cry,   Abba,   Father!
```

16 The Spirit Himself
witnesses with our
spirit, that we are chil-
dren of God.
17 And if children, also
heirs; truly heirs of God
and joint-heirs of
Christ, if indeed we suf-
fer together, that we
may also be glorified to-
gether.

```
846 3588 4151        4828       3588   4151     2257 3754 2070
16 αὐτὸ τὸ Πνεῦμα συμμαρτυρεῖ τῷ πνεύματι ἡμῶν, ὅτι ἐσμὲν
itself  The Spirit   bears witness with the spirit   of us,   that we are

5043   2316      1487 1161 5043 2532    2818        2818        3303
τέκνα Θεοῦ. 17 εἰ δὲ τέκνα, καὶ κληρονόμοι· κληρονόμοι μὲν
children of God   if  And children, also heirs;       heirs       truly

2316     4789        1161 5547    1512       4841        2443
Θεοῦ, συγκληρονόμοι δὲ Χριστοῦ· εἴπερ συμπάσχομεν, ἵνα
of God, joint-heirs   and of Christ,  if indeed  we suffer together, that

2532   4888
καὶ συνδοξασθῶμεν.
also we may be glorified together
```

16 The Spirit itself
beareth witness with
our spirit, that we are the
children of God:
17 And if children, then
heirs; heirs of God, and
joint-heirs with Christ;
if so be that we suffer
with (him), that we may
be also glorified to-
gether.

18 For I calculate that
the sufferings of the
present time (are) not
worthy (to compare to)
the coming glory to be
revealed in us.
19 For the earnest ex-
pectation of the creation
is eagerly expecting the
revelation of the sons of
God.
20 For the creation was
not willingly subjected
to vanity, but through
the (One) subjecting
(it), on hope,
21 that also the creation
itself will be freed from
the slavery;

```
3049        1063 3754 3756 514 3588     3804     3588 3568 2540
18. Λογίζομαι γὰρ ὅτι οὐκ ἄξια τὰ παθήματα τοῦ νῦν καιροῦ
I calculate  For that  not worthy the sufferings of the present time

4314 3588    3195       1391    601        1519 2248     3588 1063
πρὸς τὴν μέλλουσαν δόξαν ἀποκαλυφθῆναι εἰς ἡμᾶς. 19 ἡ γὰρ
to    the   coming    glory to be revealed   in  us.    the For

603            3588   2937     3588   602       3588 5207 3588
ἀποκαραδοκία τῆς κτίσεως τὴν ἀποκάλυψιν τῶν υἱῶν τοῦ
earnest expectation of the creation  the  revelation   of the sons

2316     553           3588 1063    3153      3588 2937    5293
Θεοῦ ἀπεκδέχεται· 20 τῇ γὰρ ματαιότητι ἡ κτίσις ὑπετάγη,
of God is eagerly expecting,   for  to vanity   the creation was subjected,

3756   1635    235 1223 3588    5293      1909 1680       3754 2532
οὐχ ἑκοῦσα, ἀλλὰ διὰ τὸν ὑποτάξαντα, ἐφ' ἐλπίδι· 21 ὅτι καὶ
not   willingly,  but  through the (One) subjecting,  on  hope,    that also

846 3588    2937        1659       575 3588    1397       3588
αὐτὴ ἡ κτίσις ἐλευθερωθήσεται ἀπὸ τῆς δουλείας, τῆς
itself the  creation   will be set free   from  the    slavery
```

18 For I reckon that the
sufferings of this pre-
sent time (are) not wor-
thy (to be compared)
with the glory which
shall be revealed in us.
19 For the earnest ex-
pectation of the creature
waiteth for the manifes-
tation of the sons of
God.
20 For the creature was
made subject to vanity,
not willingly, but by
reason of him who hath
subjected (the same) in
hope.
21 Because the creature
itself also shall be delivered from the bondage

Literal Translation

of corruption to the freedom of the glory of the children of God.

22 For we know that all the creation groans together and travails together until now 23 And not only (so), but also we ourselves having the firstfruit of the Spirit, also we ourselves groan within ourselves, eagerly expecting adoption, the redemption of our body;

24 for we were saved by hope, but hope being seen is not hope: for what anyone sees, why does he also hope? 25 But if we hope for what we do not see, through patience we eagerly expect.

26 And likewise the Spirit also joins in to help our weaknesses. For we do not know what we should pray as we ought, but the Spirit Himself intercedes on behalf of us with groanings that cannot be uttered. 27 But the (One) searching the hearts knows what (is the) mind of the Spirit, because He petitions on behalf of (the) saints according to God. 28 But we know that (to) the (ones) loving God all things work together for good, (to) those being called according to purpose; 29 because whom He foreknew, He also predestinated (to be) conformed to the image of His Son, for Him to be (the) First-born among many brothers; 30 and whom He predestinated, these He also called, and whom He called, these He also justified; and whom He justified, these He also glorified. 31 What then shall we say to these things? If God (be) for us, who (can be) against us? 32 Truly (He) who did not spare His own Son, but gave Him up on behalf of us all, how will

Greek Text (Interlinear)

5356 1519 3588 1657 3588 1391 3588 5043 3588 2316
φθορᾶς εἰς τὴν ἐλευθερίαν τῆς δόξης τῶν τέκνων τοῦ Θεοῦ
of corruption to the freedom of the glory of the children of God.

1492 1063 3754 3956 3588 2937 4959 2532 4944
22 οἴδαμεν γὰρ ὅτι πᾶσα ἡ κτίσις συστενάζει καὶ συνωδίνει
we know For that all the creation groans together and travails

891 3588 3568 3756 3440 1161 235 2532 846 3588 536
ἄχρι τοῦ νῦν· 23 οὐ μόνον δέ, ἀλλὰ καὶ αὐτοὶ τὴν ἀπαρχὴν
until the present; not only And (so), but also ourselves the firstfruit

3588 4151 2192 2532 2249 846 1722 1438 4727
τοῦ Πνεύματος ἔχοντες, καὶ ἡμεῖς αὐτοὶ ἐν ἑαυτοῖς στενά-
of the Spirit having, also we ourselves in ourselves groan,

5206 553 3588 629
ζομεν, υἱοθεσίαν ἀπεκδεχόμενοι, τὴν ἀπολύτρωσιν τοῦ
adoption eagerly expecting, the redemption of the

4983 2257 3588 1063 1680 4982 1680 1161 991
σώματος ἡμῶν. 24 τῇ γὰρ ἐλπίδι ἐσώθημεν· ἐλπὶς δὲ βλεπομένη
body of us For by hope we were being saved, hope but being seen

3756 2076 1680 3739 1063 991 5100 5101 2532 1679 1487 1161 3739
οὐκ ἔστιν ἐλπίς· ὃ γὰρ βλέπει τίς, τί καὶ ἐλπίζει; 25 εἰ δὲ ὃ
not is hope; what for sees anyone, why also does he hope? if But what

3756 991 1679 1223 5281 553
οὐ βλέπομεν ἐλπίζομεν, δι' ὑπομονῆς ἀπεκδεχόμεθα.
not we see we hope (for), through patience we eagerly expect.

5615 1161 2532 3588 4151 3588
26. Ὡσαύτως δὲ καὶ τὸ Πνεῦμα συναντιλαμβάνεται ταῖς
Likewise And also the Spirit joins in to help the

769 2257 3588 1063 5101 4336 2526 1163 3756
ἀσθενείαις ἡμῶν· τὸ γὰρ τί προσευξώμεθα καθὸ δεῖ, οὐκ
weaknesses of us; for what we may pray (for) as we ought, not

1492 235 846 3588 4151 5241 5228 2257
οἴδαμεν, ἀλλ' αὐτὸ τὸ πνεῦμα ὑπερεντυγχάνει ὑπὲρ ἡμῶν
we know, but itself the Spirit intercedes on behalf of us

4726 215 3588 1161 2045 3588 2588 1492 5101 3588
στεναγμοῖς ἀλαλήτοις· 27 ὁ δὲ ἐραυνῶν τὰς καρδίας οἶδε τί τὸ
with groanings unutterable; the (One) but searching the hearts knows what

5427 3588 4151 3754 2596 2316 1793 5228
φρόνημα τοῦ Πνεύματος, ὅτι κατὰ Θεὸν ἐντυγχάνει ὑπὲρ
(is the) mind of the Spirit, because according to God He petitions on behalf of

40 1492 1161 3754 3588 25 3588 2316 3956 4903
ἁγίων. 28 οἴδαμεν δὲ ὅτι τοῖς ἀγαπῶσι τὸν Θεὸν πάντα συν-
saints we know And that the (ones) loving God all things

1519 18 3588 2596 4286 2822 5607 3754 3739
εργεῖ εἰς ἀγαθόν, τοῖς κατὰ πρόθεσιν κλητοῖς οὖσιν. 29 ὅτι οὓς
work together for good, those according to purpose called out being. For whom

4309 2532 4309 5656 3588 1504 3588 5207
προέγνω, καὶ προώρισε συμμόρφους τῆς εἰκόνος τοῦ υἱοῦ
He foreknew, also He predestinated conformed to the image of the Son

846 1519 3588 1511 846 4416 1722 4183 80
αὐτοῦ, εἰς τὸ εἶναι αὐτὸν πρωτότοκον ἐν πολλοῖς ἀδελφοῖς·
of Him, for to be Him First-born among many brothers;

3739 1161 4309 5128 2532 2564 2532 3739 2564
30 οὓς δὲ προώρισε, τούτους καὶ ἐκάλεσε· καὶ οὓς ἐκάλεσε, τού-
whom; and He predestinated these also He called; and whom He called,

5128 2532 1344 3739 1161 1344 5128 2532 1392
τους καὶ ἐδικαίωσεν· οὓς δὲ ἐδικαίωσε, τούτους καὶ ἐδόξασε.
these also He justified; whom and He justified, these also He glorified

5101 3767 2046 4314 5023 1487 3588 2316 5228 2257 5101
31. Τί οὖν ἐροῦμεν πρὸς ταῦτα; εἰ ὁ Θεὸς ὑπὲρ ἡμῶν, τίς
what Then shall we say to these things? If God (be) for us, who

2596 2257 3739 1065 3588 2398 5207 3756 5339 235 5228
καθ' ἡμῶν; 32 ὅς γε τοῦ ἰδίου υἱοῦ οὐκ ἐφείσατο, ἀλλ' ὑπὲρ
against us? (He) who truly the own Son not spared, but on behalf of

King James Version

of corruption into the glorious liberty of the children of God.

22 For we know that the whole creation groaneth and travaileth in pain together until now.

23 And not only (they), but ourselves also, which have the firstfruits of the Spirit, even we ourselves groan within ourselves, waiting for the adoption, (to wit), the redemption of our body.

24 For we are saved by hope: but hope that is seen is not hope: for what a man seeth, why doth he yet hope for? 25 But if we hope for that we see not, (then) do we with patience wait for (it).

26 Likewise the Spirit also helpeth our infirmities: for we know not what we should pray for as we ought: but the Spirit itself maketh intercession for us with groanings which cannot be uttered. 27 And he that searcheth the hearts knoweth what (is) the mind of the Spirit, because he maketh intercession for the saints according to (the will of) God. 28 And we know that all things work together for good to them that love God, to them who are the called according to (his) purpose. 29 For whom he did foreknow, he also did predestinate (to be) conformed to the image of his Son, that he might be the firstborn among many brethren. 30 Moreover whom he did predestinate, them he also called: and whom he called, them he also justified: and whom he justified, them he also glorified. 31 What shall we then say to these things? If God (be) for us, who (can be) against us? 32 He that spared not his own Son, but delivered him up for us all, how shall

Romans 8:33

Literal Translation

He not freely give all things with Him to us?

33 Who will bring (any) charge against God's elect? God (is) the (One) justifying!
34 Who (is) the (one) condemning? Christ (is) the (One) having died, but rather also having been raised, who also is at (the) right (hand) of God, who also intercedes on our behalf!
35 Who shall separate us from the love of Christ? (Shall) tribulation, or distress, or persecution, or famine, or nakedness, or danger, or sword?
36 Even as it has been written, "For Your sake we are killed all the day; we are counted as sheep of slaughter." (Psa 44:22)
37 But in all these things we more than conquer through the (One) loving us.
38 For I have been persuaded that neither death, nor life, nor angels, nor rulers, nor powers, nor things present, nor things coming, 39 nor height, nor depth, nor any other creature will be able to separate us from the love of God in Christ Jesus, our Lord.

Greek Interlinear

2257 3956 3860 846 4459 3780 2532 4862 846
ἡμῶν πάντων παρέδωκεν αὐτόν, πῶς οὐχὶ καὶ σὺν αὐτῷ
us all gave up Him, how not also with Him

3588 3956 2254 5483 5101 1458 2596 1588
τὰ πάντα ἡμῖν χαρίσεται; 33 τίς ἐγκαλέσει κατὰ ἐκλεκτῶν
all things to us will He freely give? Who will bring charge against the elect

2316 2316 3588 1344 5101 3588 2632 5547 3588
Θεοῦ; Θεὸς ὁ δικαιῶν· 34 τίς ὁ κατακρινῶν; Χριστὸς ὁ ἀπο-
of God? God (is) He justifying; who (is) he condemning? Christ (is) the (One)

599 3123 1161 2532 1453 3739 2532 2076 1722 1188 3588
θανών, μᾶλλον δὲ καὶ ἐγερθείς, ὃς καί ἐστιν ἐν δεξιᾷ τοῦ
having died, rather but also having been raised, who also is at (the) right

2316 3739 2532 1793 5228 2257 5101 2248 5563 575
Θεοῦ, ὃς καὶ ἐντυγχάνει ὑπὲρ ἡμῶν. 35 τίς ἡμᾶς χωρίσει ἀπὸ
of God, who also intercedes on behalf of us. Who us will separate from

3588 26 3588 5547 2347 2228 4730 2228 1375 2228
τῆς ἀγάπης τοῦ Χριστοῦ; θλῖψις, ἢ στενοχωρία, ἢ διωγμός, ἢ
the love of Christ? (Shall) trouble, or distress, or persecution, or

3042 2228 1132 2228 2794 2228 3162 2531 1125
λιμός, ἢ γυμνότης, ἢ κίνδυνος, ἢ μάχαιρα; 36 καθὼς γέγραπται
famine, or nakedness, or danger, or sword? Even as it has been written,

3754 1752 4675 2289 3650 3588 2250 3049
ὅτι Ἕνεκεά σου θανατούμεθα ὅλην τὴν ἡμέραν ἐλυγίσθημεν
For the sake of You we are being killed all the day; we were counted

5613 4263 4967 235 1722 5125 3956 5245 1223
ὡς πρόβατα σφαγῆς. 37 ἀλλ ἐν τούτοις πᾶσιν ὑπερνικῶμεν διὰ
as sheep of slaughter. But in these things all we overconquer through

3588 25 2248 3982 1063 3754 3777 2288
τοῦ ἀγαπήσαντος ἡμᾶς. 38 πέπεισμαι γὰρ ὅτι οὔτε θάνατος
the (One) loving us I have been persuaded For that not death

3777 2222 3777 32 3777 746 3777 1411 3777 1764
οὔτε ζωὴ οὔτε ἄγγελοι οὔτε ἀρχαὶ οὔτε δυνάμεις οὔτε ἐνεστῶτα
nor life nor angels nor rulers nor powers nor things present

3777 3195 3777 5313 3777 899 3777 5100 2937 2087
οὔτε μέλλοντα 39 οὔτε ὕψωμα οὔτε βάθος οὔτε τις κτίσις ἑτέρα
nor things coming nor height nor depth nor any creature other

1410 2248 5563 575 3588 26 3588 2316 3588 1722
δυνήσεται ἡμᾶς χωρίσαι ἀπὸ τῆς ἀγάπης τοῦ Θεοῦ τῆς ἐν
will be able us to separate from the love of God in

5547 2424 3588 2962 2257
Χριστῷ Ἰησοῦ τῷ Κυρίῳ ἡμῶν.
Christ Jesus the Lord of us.

he not with him also freely give us all things?

33 Who shall lay any thing to the charge of God's elect? (It is) God that justifieth.
34 Who (is) he that condemneth? (It is) Christ that died, yea rather, that is risen again, who is even at the right hand of God, who also maketh intercession for us.
35 Who shall separate us from the love of Christ? (shall) tribulation, or distress, or persecution, or famine, or peril, or sword?
36 As it is written, For thy sake we are killed all the day long; we are accounted as sheep for the slaughter.
37 Nay, in all these things we are more than conquerors through him that loved us.
38 For I am persuaded, that neither death, nor life, nor angels, nor principalities, nor powers, nor things present, nor things to come,
39 Nor height, nor depth, nor any other creature, shall be able to separate us from the love of God, which is in Christ Jesus our Lord

Acrostic Index

The following is the full chapter, in English and in Greek of Galations: Chapter 3, Verse 27, where acrostic 9 begins, is clearly marked.

1. O foolish Galatians, who bewitched you not to obey the truth, to whom before (your) eyes Jesus Christ was written afore among you crucified?

2 This only I desire to learn from you: Did you receive the Spirit by works of law or by hearing of faith?

3 Are you so foolish? Having begun in (the) Spirit, do you now perfect (yourself) in the flesh?

4 Did you suffer so much vainly, if indeed (it) also (was) vainly?

5 Then He supplying the Spirit to you and working works of power in you, (is it) by works of law, or by hearing of faith?

6 Even as Abraham believed God, and it was counted to him for righteousness,

7 know, then, that those of faith, these are sons of Abraham.

8 And the Scripture foreseeing that God would justify the nations by faith, preached the gospel before to Abraham: "All the nations will be blessed in you." (Gen 12:3)

9 So that those of faith are blessed with

5599 453 1052 5101 5209 940 3588 225 3361
1. Ὦ ἀνόητοι Γαλάται, τίς ὑμᾶς ἐβάσκανε τῇ ἀληθείᾳ μὴ
O foolish Galatians, who you bewitched the truth not

3982 3739 2596 3788 2424 5547 4270
πείθεσθαι, οἷς κατ' ὀφθαλμοὺς Ἰησοῦς Χριστὸς προεγράφη
to obey. to whom before the eyes of Jesus Christ was written afore

1722 5213 4717 5124 3440 2309 3129 575 5216
ἐν ὑμῖν ἐσταυρωμένος; 2 τοῦτο μόνον θέλω μαθεῖν ἀφ' ὑμῶν,
among you crucified? This only I desire to learn from you,

1537 2041 3551 3588 4151 2983 2228 1537 189 4102
ἐξ ἔργων νόμου τὸ Πνεῦμα ἐλάβετε, ἢ ἐξ ἀκοῆς πίστεως;
by works of law the Spirit did you receive, or by hearing of faith?

3779 453 2075 1728 4151 3568 4561
3 οὕτως ἀνόητοί ἐστε; ἐναρξάμενοι Πνεύματι, νῦν σαρκὶ
so foolish Are you? having begun in (the) Spirit, now (in) flesh

2005 5118 3958 1500 -1489- 2532 1500 3588 3767
ἐπιτελεῖσθε; 4 τοσαῦτα ἐπάθετε εἰκῇ; εἴ γε καὶ εἰκῇ. 5 ὁ οὖν
do you perfect? So much suffered you vainly? If indeed even vainly. He then

2023 5213 3588 4151 2532 1754 1411 1722 5213
ἐπιχορηγῶν ὑμῖν τὸ Πνεῦμα καὶ ἐνεργῶν δυνάμεις ἐν ὑμῖν,
supplying to you the Spirit and working works of power in you,

1537 2041 3551 2228 1537 189 4102 2531 11
ἐξ ἔργων νόμου, ἢ ἐξ ἀκοῆς πίστεως; 6 καθὼς Ἀβραὰμ ἐπί-
by works of law, or by hearing of faith? Even as Abraham

4100 3588 2316 2532 3049 846 1519 1343 1097
στευσε τῷ Θεῷ, καὶ ἐλογίσθη αὐτῷ εἰς δικαιοσύνην. 7 γινώ-
believed God, and it was counted to him for righteousness. Know

686 3754 3588 1537 4102 3778 1526 5207 11
σκετε ἄρα ὅτι οἱ ἐκ πίστεως, οὗτοί εἰσιν υἱοὶ Ἀβραάμ.
then that those of faith, these are sons of Abraham.

4275 1161 3588 1124 3754 1537 4102 1344 3588 1484 3588
8 προϊδοῦσα δὲ ἡ γραφὴ ὅτι ἐκ πίστεως δικαιοῖ τὰ ἔθνη ὁ
foreseeing And the Scripture that by faith would justify the nations

2316 4283 3588 11 3754 2127
Θεός, προευηγγελίσατο τῷ Ἀβραὰμ ὅτι Εὐλογηθήσονται
God. preached the gospel before to Abraham that will be blessed

1722 4671 3956 3588 1484 5620 3588 1537 4102 2127 4862
ἐν σοὶ πάντα τὰ ἔθνη. 9 ὥστε οἱ ἐκ πίστεως εὐλογοῦνται σὺν
in you all the nations. So as those of faith are blessed with

---

1. O foolish Galatians, who hath bewitched you, that ye should not obey the truth, before whose eyes Jesus Christ hath been evidently set forth, crucified among you?

2 This only would I learn of you, Received ye the Spirit by the works of the law, or by the hearing of faith?

3 Are ye so foolish? having begun in the Spirit, are ye now made perfect by the flesh?

4 Have ye suffered so many things in vain? if (it be) yet in vain.

5 He therefore that ministereth to you the Spirit, and worketh miracles among you, (doeth he it) by the works of the law, or by the hearing of faith?

6 Even as Abraham believed God, and it was accounted to him for righteousness.

7 Know ye therefore that they which are of faith, the same are the children of Abraham.

8 And the scripture, foreseeing that God would justify the heathen through faith, preached before the gospel unto Abraham, (saying,) In thee shall all nations be blessed.

9 So then they which be of faith are blessed with

Galatians 3:10

Literal Translation   **King James Version**

Literal Translation

the faithful Abraham. 10 For as many as are out of works of law, (these) are under a curse. For it has been written, "Cursed (is) everyone who does not continue in all the things having been written in the book of the Law, to do them." (Deut. 27:26) 11 And that no one is justified by law before God (is) clear because, "The just shall live by faith." (Hab. 2:4) 12 But the Law is not of faith, but, "The man doing these things shall live in them." (Lev. 18:5) 13 Christ redeemed us from the curse of the law, having become a curse for us: for it has been written, "Cursed (is) everyone having been hung on a tree." (Deut. 21:23) 14 that the blessing of Abraham might be to the nations in Christ Jesus, that we might receive the promise of the Spirit through faith.

15 Brothers, I speak according to man, a covenant having been ratified, even (among) mankind, no one sets aside or adds to (it). 16 But the promises were spoken to Abraham and to his Seed (it does not say, And to seeds, as of many, but as of one, "And to your Seed," which is Christ). (Gen. 3:15; 21:12; 22:18; 24:7) 17 And I say this, A covenant having been ratified before to Christ by God, (the) Law coming into being four hundred and thirty years after, does not annul the promise, so as to abolish (it). 18 For if the inheritance (is) of law, (it is) no more of promise; but God has given (it) to Abraham through promise. 19 Why the Law then? It was added for the sake of transgressions,

Greek text

τῷ πιστῷ Ἀβραάμ. 10 ὅσοι γὰρ ἐξ ἔργων νόμου εἰσίν, ὑπὸ κατάραν εἰσί· γέγραπται γάρ, Ἐπικατάρατος πᾶς ὃς οὐκ ἐμμένει ἐν πᾶσι τοῖς γεγραμμένοις ἐν τῷ βιβλίῳ τοῦ νόμου, τοῦ ποιῆσαι αὐτά. 11 ὅτι δὲ ἐν νόμῳ οὐδεὶς δικαιοῦται παρὰ τῷ Θεῷ, δῆλον· ὅτι Ὁ δίκαιος ἐκ πίστεως ζήσεται· 12 ὁ δὲ νόμος οὐκ ἔστιν ἐκ πίστεως, ἀλλ' Ὁ ποιήσας αὐτὰ ἄνθρωπος ζήσεται ἐν αὐτοῖς. 13 Χριστὸς ἡμᾶς ἐξηγόρασεν ἐκ τῆς κατάρας τοῦ νόμου, γενόμενος ὑπὲρ ἡμῶν κατάρα· γέγραπται γάρ, Ἐπικατάρατος πᾶς ὁ κρεμάμενος ἐπὶ ξύλου· 14 ἵνα εἰς τὰ ἔθνη ἡ εὐλογία τοῦ Ἀβραὰμ γένηται ἐν Χριστῷ Ἰησοῦ, ἵνα τὴν ἐπαγγελίαν τοῦ Πνεύματος λάβωμεν διὰ τῆς πίστεως.

15 Ἀδελφοί, κατὰ ἄνθρωπον λέγω· ὅμως ἀνθρώπου κεκυρωμένην διαθήκην οὐδεὶς ἀθετεῖ ἢ ἐπιδιατάσσεται. 16 τῷ δὲ Ἀβραὰμ ἐρρήθησαν αἱ ἐπαγγελίαι, καὶ τῷ σπέρματι αὐτοῦ. οὐ λέγει, Καὶ τοῖς σπέρμασιν, ὡς ἐπὶ πολλῶν, ἀλλ' ὡς ἐφ' ἑνός, Καὶ τῷ σπέρματί σου, ὅς ἐστι Χριστός. 17 τοῦτο δὲ λέγω, διαθήκην προκεκυρωμένην ὑπὸ τοῦ Θεοῦ εἰς Χριστὸν ὁ μετὰ ἔτη τετρακόσια καὶ τριάκοντα γεγονὼς νόμος οὐκ ἀκυροῖ, εἰς τὸ καταργῆσαι τὴν ἐπαγγελίαν. 18 εἰ γὰρ ἐκ νόμου ἡ κληρονομία, οὐκέτι ἐξ ἐπαγγελίας· τῷ δὲ Ἀβραὰμ δι' ἐπαγγελίας κεχάρισται ὁ Θεός. 19 τί οὖν ὁ νόμος; τῶν παραβάσεων χάριν

King James Version

faithful Abraham. 10 For as many as are of the works of the law are under the curse: for it is written, Cursed (is) every one that continueth not in all things which are written in the book of the law to do them. 11 But that no man is justified by the law in the sight of God, (it is) evident: for, The just shall live by faith. 12 And the law is not of faith: but, The man that doeth them shall live in them. 13 Christ hath redeemed us from the curse of the law, being made a curse for us: for it is written, Cursed (is) every one that hangeth on a tree: 14 That the blessing of Abraham might come on the Gentiles through Jesus Christ; that we might receive the promise of the Spirit through faith. 15 Brethren, I speak after the manner of men; Though (it be) but a man's covenant, yet (if it be) confirmed, no man disannulleth, or addeth thereto. 16 Now to Abraham and his seed were the promises made. He saith not, And to seeds, as of many; but as of one, And to thy seed, which is Christ. 17 And this I say, (that) the covenant, that was confirmed before of God in Christ, the law, which was four hundred and thirty years after, cannot disannul, that it should make the promise of none effect. 18 For if the inheritance (be) of the law, (it is) no more of promise: but God gave (it) to Abraham by promise. 19 Wherefore then (serveth) the law? It was added because of transgressions,

Galatians 3:20

Literal Translation (left) · Greek Interlinear (center) · *King James Version* (right)

Literal Translation

until the Seed should have come, to whom it had been promised, being ordained through angels in a mediator's hand. 20 But the Mediator is not of one, but God is one. 21 Then is the Law against the promises of God? Let it not be! For if a law had been given which had been able to make alive, indeed righteousness would have been out of law. 22 But the Scripture locked up all under sin, that the promise by faith of Jesus Christ might be given to the ones believing.

23 But before the coming of faith, we were guarded under law, having been locked up to the faith being about to be revealed. 24 So that the Law has become a trainer of us (until) Christ, that we might be justified by faith. 25 But faith having come, we are no longer under a trainer. 26 For you are all sons of God through faith in Christ Jesus. 27 For as many as were baptized into Christ, you put on Christ. 28 There is not Jew nor Greek, there is no slave nor freeman, there is no male and female; for you are all one in Christ Jesus. 29 And if you (are) of Christ, then you are a seed of Abraham, even heirs according to promise.

Greek Interlinear

4369 891 3752 2064 3588 4690 3739 1861 1299
προσετέθη, ἄχρις οὗ ἔλθῃ τὸ σπέρμα ᾧ ἐπήγγελται, διατα-
it was added, until should have come the Seed to whom it has been made, having

1223 32 1722 5495 3316 3588 1161 3316 1520 3756
γεὶς δι' ἀγγέλων ἐν χειρὶ μεσίτου. 20 ὁ δὲ μεσίτης ἑνὸς οὐκ
been ordained through angels in hand a mediator's. the But mediator of one not

2076 3588 1161 2316 1520 2076 3588 3767 3551 2596 3588 1860
ἔστιν. ὁ δὲ Θεὸς εἷς ἐστιν. 21 ὁ οὖν νόμος κατὰ τῶν ἐπαγγελιῶν
is. but God one is. the Then Law against the promises

3588 2316 3361 1096 1487 1063 1325 3551 3588 1410
τοῦ Θεοῦ; μὴ γένοιτο. εἰ γὰρ ἐδόθη νόμος ὁ δυνάμενος
of God (is)? Not let it be! if For has been given a law which was able

2227 3689 3021 537 3551 2258 3588 1343 235
ζωοποιῆσαι, ὄντως ἂν ἐκ νόμου ἦν ἡ δικαιοσύνη. 22 ἀλλὰ
to make alive, indeed would out of law been the righteousness. But

4788 3588 1124 3588 3956 5259 266 2443/3588
συνέκλεισεν ἡ γραφὴ τὰ πάντα ὑπὸ ἁμαρτίαν, ἵνα ἡ
locked up the Scriptures all under sin, that the

1860 1537 4102 2424 5547 1325 3588 4100
ἐπαγγελία ἐκ πίστεως Ἰησοῦ Χριστοῦ δοθῇ τοῖς πιστεύουσι.
promise by faith of Jesus Christ might be given to those believing.

4253 3588 1161 2064 3588 4102 5259 3551 5432
23 Πρὸ τοῦ δὲ ἐλθεῖν τὴν πίστιν, ὑπὸ νόμον ἐφρουρούμεθα,
before the But coming of faith, under law we were guarded,

4788 1519 3588 3195 4102 601
συγκεκλεισμένοι εἰς τὴν μέλλουσαν πίστιν ἀποκαλυφθῆναι.
having been locked up to the being about faith to be revealed.

2620 3588 3551 3807 2257 1096 1519 5547 2443
24 ὥστε ὁ νόμος παιδαγωγὸς ἡμῶν γέγονεν εἰς Χριστόν, ἵνα
So as the law a trainer of us has become (until) Christ, that

1537 4102 1344 2064 1161 3588 4102 3765
ἐκ πίστεως δικαιωθῶμεν. 25 ἐλθούσης δὲ τῆς πίστεως, οὐκέτι
by faith we might be justified. having come But faith, no more

5259 3807 2070 3956 1063 5207 2316 2075 1223 3588
ὑπὸ παιδαγωγόν ἐσμεν. 26 πάντες γὰρ υἱοὶ Θεοῦ ἐστὲ διὰ τῆς
under a trainer we are. all For sons of God you are through

4102 1722 5547 2424 3745 1063 1519 5547 907
πίστεως ἐν Χριστῷ Ἰησοῦ. (27) ὅσοι γὰρ εἰς Χριστὸν ἐβαπτί-
faith in Christ Jesus. as many as For into Christ were

5547 1746 3756 1762 2453 3761 1672
σθητε, Χριστὸν ἐνεδύσασθε. 28 οὐκ ἔνι Ἰουδαῖος οὐδὲ Ἕλλην,
baptized, Christ you put on. not There is Jew nor Greek,

3756 1762 1401 3761 1658 3756 1762 730 2532 2338 3956
οὐκ ἔνι δοῦλος οὐδὲ ἐλεύθερος, οὐκ ἔνι ἄρσεν καὶ θῆλυ· πάντες
not there is slave nor freeman, not there is male and female; all

1063 5210 1519 2075 1722 5547 2424 1487 1161 5210 5547
γὰρ ὑμεῖς εἷς ἐστὲ ἐν Χριστῷ Ἰησοῦ. 29 εἰ δὲ ὑμεῖς Χριστοῦ,
for you one are in Christ Jesus. if And you (are) of Christ,

686 3588 11 4690 2075 2532 2596 1860 2818
ἄρα τοῦ Ἀβραὰμ σπέρμα ἐστέ, καὶ κατ' ἐπαγγελίαν κληρονό-
then of Abraham a seed you are, even according to promise heirs

μοι.

King James Version

till the seed should come to whom the promise was made; (and it was) ordained by angels in the hand of a mediator. 20 Now a mediator is not (a mediator) of one, but God is one. 21 (Is) the law then against the promises of God? God forbid: for if there had been a law given which could have given life, verily righteousness should have been by the law. 22 But the scripture hath concluded all under sin, that the promise by faith of Jesus Christ might be given to them that believe.

23 But before faith came, we were kept under the law, shut up unto the faith which should afterwards be revealed. 24 Wherefore the law was our schoolmaster (to bring us) unto Christ, that we might be justified by faith. 25 But after that faith is come, we are no longer under a schoolmaster. 26 For ye are all the children of God by faith in Christ Jesus. 27 For as many of you as have been baptized into Christ have put on Christ. 28 There is neither Jew nor Greek, there is neither bond nor free, there is neither male nor female: for ye are all one in Christ Jesus. 29 And if ye (be) Christ's, then are ye Abraham's seed, and heirs according to the promise.

Galatians 4

Literal Translation

1. But I say, Over so long a time the heir is an infant, he being lord of all, does not differ from a slave. 2 but is under

Greek Interlinear

3004 1161 1909 3745 5550 3588 2818 3516 2076 3516 2076
1. Λέγω δέ, ἐφ' ὅσον χρόνον ὁ κληρονόμος νήπιός ἐστιν,
I say But over so long a time the heir an infant is,

3762 1308 1401 2962 3956 5607 235 5259
οὐδὲν διαφέρει δούλου, κύριος πάντων ὤν· 2 ἀλλὰ ὑπὸ
nothing he differs (from) a slave, lord of all being, but under

King James Version

1. Now I say, (That) the heir, as long as he is a child, differeth nothing from a servant, though he be lord of all; 2 But is under

Acrostic Index

The following is the full chapter, in English and in Greek of Colossians: Chapter 3, Verse 11, where acrostic 10 begins, is clearly marked.

1. If, then, you were raised with Christ, seek the things above, where Christ is sitting at (the) right of God.
2 mind the things above, not the things on the earth,
3 For you died, and your life has been hidden with Christ in God.
4 Whenever Christ our life is revealed, then also you will be revealed with Him in glory.

5 Then put to death your members which (are) on the earth: fornication, uncleanness, passion; evil lust; and covetousness, which is idolatry;
6 on account of which things the wrath of God is coming on the sons of disobedience,
7 among whom you also walked at one time, when you lived in these.
8 But now, you also, put off all (these) things: wrath, anger, malice, evil-speaking, shameful speech

---

1487 3767 4591 3588 5547 3588 507 2212 3757/3588
1. Εἰ οὖν συνηγέρθητε τῷ Χριστῷ, τὰ ἄνω ζητεῖτε, οὗ ὁ
   If then you were raised with Christ, the things above seek, where

5547 2076 1722 1188 3588 2316 2521 3588 507
Χριστός ἐστιν ἐν δεξιᾷ τοῦ Θεοῦ καθήμενος. 2 τὰ ἄνω
Christ   is   at (the) right of God sitting   the things above

5426 3361 3588 1909 3588 1093 599 1063 2532 3588 2222 5216
φρονεῖτε, μὴ τὰ ἐπὶ τῆς γῆς. 3 ἀπεθάνετε γάρ, καὶ ἡ ζωὴ ὑμῶν
Mind,   not the things on the earth you died   For, and the life of you

2928 4862 3588 5547 1722 3588 2316 3752 3588 5547
κέκρυπται σὺν τῷ Χριστῷ ἐν τῷ Θεῷ. 4 ὅταν ὁ Χριστὸς
has been hidden with Christ   in God. Whenever   Christ

5319 3588 2222 2257 5119 2532 5210 4862 846
φανερωθῇ, ἡ ζωὴ ἡμῶν, τότε καὶ ὑμεῖς σὺν αὐτῷ
is revealed, the life of us, then also you   with Him

5319 1722 1391
φανερωθήσεσθε ἐν δόξῃ.
will be revealed in glory.

3499 3767 3588 3196 5216 3588 1909 3588 1093 4202
5. Νεκρώσατε οὖν τὰ μέλη ὑμῶν τὰ ἐπὶ τῆς γῆς, πορνείαν,
put to death Therefore the members of you on the earth, fornication,

167 3806 1939 2556 2532 3588 4124
ἀκαθαρσίαν, πάθος, ἐπιθυμίαν κακήν, καὶ τὴν πλεονεξίαν,
uncleanness, passion, lust   evil, and   covetousness.

3748 2076 1495 1223 3739 2064 3588 3709 3588 2316
ἥτις ἐστὶν εἰδωλολατρεία, 6 δι' ἃ ἔρχεται ἡ ὀργὴ τοῦ Θεοῦ
which is   idolatry;   because of which is coming the wrath of God

1909 3588 5207 3588 543 1722 3739 2532 5210 4043
ἐπὶ τοὺς υἱοὺς τῆς ἀπειθείας· 7 ἐν οἷς καὶ ὑμεῖς περιεπατήσατέ
on   the sons of disobedience; among whom also you   walked

4218 3753 2198 1722 846 3570 1161 659 2532 5210 3588
ποτε, ὅτε ἐζῆτε ἐν αὐτοῖς. 8 νυνὶ δὲ ἀπόθεσθε καὶ ὑμεῖς τὰ
then, when you lived in these.   now But put off   also you

3956 3709 2372 2549 988 148
πάντα, ὀργήν, θυμόν, κακίαν, βλασφημίαν, αἰσχρολογίαν
all things wrath, anger, malice, evil speaking, shameful speech

---

1. If ye then be risen with Christ, seek those things which are above, where Christ sitteth on the right hand of God.
2 Set your affection on things above, not on things on the earth.
3 For ye are dead, and your life is hid with Christ in God.
4 When Christ, (who is) our life, shall appear, then shall ye also appear with him in glory.

5 Mortify therefore your members which are upon the earth; fornication, uncleanness, inordinate affection, evil concupiscence, and covetousness, which is idolatry:
6 For which things' sake the wrath of God cometh on the children of disobedience:
7 In the which ye also walked some time, when ye lived in them.
8 But now ye also put off all these; anger, wrath, malice, blasphemy, filthy communication

Literal Translation	Colossians 3:9	King James Version

Literal Translation (left column):

out of your mouth.
9 Do not lie to one another, having put off the old man with his practices.

10 and having put on the new, having been renewed in full knowledge according to (the) image of the (One) creating him.
11 Where there is no Greek and Jew, circumcision and uncircumcision, foreigner, Scythian, slave, (or) freeman, but Christ (is) all things and in all.

12 Then put on as elect ones of God, holy and being loved, bowels of compassions, kindness, humility, meekness, long-suffering.

13 bearing with one another and forgiving yourselves, if anyone has a complaint against any, even as Christ forgave you, so also you (should forgive);
14 And above all these (add) love, which is (the) bond of perfectness.

15 And let the peace of God rule in your hearts, to which you also were called in one body, and be thankful.
16 Let the Word of Christ dwell in you richly, in all wisdom teaching and exhorting yourselves in psalms and hymns and spiritual songs, singing with grace in your hearts to the Lord.

17 And everything whatever you do in word or in work, (do) all things in the name of (the) Lord Jesus, giving thanks to God and (the) Father through Him.

18 Wives, be subject to (your) own husbands, as is becoming.

Interlinear (center column):

1537 3588 4750 5216 3361 5574 1519 240 554
Ἐκ τοῦ στόματος ὑμῶν· 9 μὴ ψεύδεσθε εἰς ἀλλήλους, ἀπεκδυσά-
out of the mouth of you; Not do lie to one another, having put

3588 3820 444 4862 3588 4234 846
μενοι τὸν παλαιὸν ἄνθρωπον σὺν ταῖς πράξεσιν αὐτοῦ,
off the old man with the practices of him.

2532 1746 3588 3501 3588 341 1519
10 καὶ ἐνδυσάμενοι τὸν νέον, τὸν ἀνακαινούμενον εἰς
and having put on the new (man), being renewed in

1922 2596 1504 3588 2936 846 3699 3756 1762
ἐπίγνωσιν κατ' εἰκόνα τοῦ κτίσαντος αὐτόν· 11 ὅπου οὐκ ἔνι
knowledge according to image of the (One) creating him; where not there is

1672 2532 2453 4061 2532 203 915
Ἕλλην καὶ Ἰουδαῖος, περιτομὴ καὶ ἀκροβυστία, βάρβαρος,
Greek and Jew, circumcision and uncircumcision, foreigner,

4658 1401 1658 235 3588 3956 2532 1722 3956 5547
Σκύθης, δοῦλος, ἐλεύθερος· ἀλλὰ τὰ πάντα καὶ ἐν πᾶσι Χριστός.
Scythian, slave, (or) freeman, but all things and in all Christ (is).

1746 3767 5613 1588 3588 2316 40 2532
12. Ἐνδύσασθε οὖν, ὡς ἐκλεκτοὶ τοῦ Θεοῦ, ἅγιοι καὶ
put on Therefore, as elect ones of God, holy and

25 4698 3628 5544 501
ἠγαπημένοι, σπλάγχνα οἰκτιρμῶν, χρηστότητα, ταπεινο-
being loved, bowels of compassions, kindness, humility,

4236 3115 430 240
φροσύνην, πραότητα, μακροθυμίαν· 13 ἀνεχόμενοι ἀλλήλων,
meekness, long-suffering, forbearing one another,

2532 5483 1438 1437 5100 4314 5100 2192 3437 2531
καὶ χαριζόμενοι ἑαυτοῖς, ἐάν τις πρός τινα ἔχῃ μομφήν· καθὼς
and forgiving yourselves, if anyone against any has a complaint, as

2532 3588 5547 5483 5213 3779 2532 5210 1909 3956 1161
καὶ ὁ Χριστὸς ἐχαρίσατο ὑμῖν, οὕτω καὶ ὑμεῖς· 14 ἐπὶ πᾶσι δὲ
indeed Christ forgave you, so also you, above all and

5125 3588 26 3748 2076 4886 3588 5047
τούτοις τὴν ἀγάπην, ἥτις ἐστὶ σύνδεσμος τῆς τελειότητος.
these things love, which is (the) bond of perfectness.

2532 3588 1515 3588 2316 1018 1722 3588 2588 5216
15 καὶ ἡ εἰρήνη τοῦ Θεοῦ βραβευέτω ἐν ταῖς καρδίαις ὑμῶν,
And the peace of God let rule in the hearts of you,

1519 3739 2532 2564 1722 1520 4983 2532 2170 1096 3588
εἰς ἣν καὶ ἐκλήθητε ἐν ἑνὶ σώματι· καὶ εὐχάριστοι γίνεσθε. 16 ὁ
to which also you were called in one body, and thankful be The

3056 3588 5547 1774 1722 5213 4146 1722 3956
λόγος τοῦ Χριστοῦ ἐνοικείτω ἐν ὑμῖν πλουσίως ἐν πάσῃ
Word of Christ let dwell in you richly in all

4678 1321 2532 3560 1438 5568 2532
σοφίᾳ· διδάσκοντες καὶ νουθετοῦντες ἑαυτούς, ψαλμοῖς, καὶ
wisdom teaching and exhorting yourselves, in Psalms, and

5215 2532 5603 4152 1722 5485 103 1722/3588
ὕμνοις, καὶ ᾠδαῖς πνευματικαῖς, ἐν χάριτι ᾄδοντες ἐν τῇ
hymns, and songs spiritual, with grace singing in the

2588 5216 3588 2962 2532 3956 3739 5100 302 4160 1722
καρδίᾳ ὑμῶν τῷ Κυρίῳ. 17 καὶ πᾶν ὅ τι ἂν ποιῆτε, ἐν
hearts of you to the Lord. And everything whatever you do, in

3056 2228 1722 2041 3956 1722 3686 2962 2424
λόγῳ ἢ ἐν ἔργῳ, πάντα ἐν ὀνόματι Κυρίου Ἰησοῦ,
word or in work, all things in (the) name of (the) Lord Jesus,

2168 3588 2316 2532 3962 1223 846
εὐχαριστοῦντες τῷ Θεῷ καὶ πατρὶ δι' αὐτοῦ.
giving thanks to God and (the) Father through Him

3588 1135 5293 3588 2398 435 5613
18. Αἱ γυναῖκες, ὑποτάσσεσθε τοῖς ἰδίοις ἀνδράσιν, ὡς
The wives, be subject to the own husbands, as

King James Version (right column):

out of your mouth.
9 Lie not one to another, seeing that ye have put off the old man with his deeds;

10 And have put on the new (man), which is renewed in knowledge after the image of him that created him:
11 Where there is neither Greek nor Jew, circumcision nor uncircumcision, Barbarian, Scythian, bond (nor) free: but Christ (is) all, and in all.

12 Put on therefore, as the elect of God, holy and beloved, bowels of mercies, kindness, humbleness of mind, meekness, longsuffering;
13 Forbearing one another, and forgiving one another, if any man have a quarrel against any: even as Christ forgave you, so also (do) ye.
14 And above all these things (put on) charity, which is the bond of perfectness.

15 And let the peace of God rule in your hearts, to the which also ye are called in one body, and be ye thankful.
16 Let the word of Christ dwell in you richly in all wisdom; teaching and admonishing one another in psalms and hymns and spiritual songs, singing with grace in your hearts to the Lord.

17 And whatsoever ye do in word or deed, (do) all in the name of the Lord Jesus, giving thanks to God and the Father by him

18 Wives, submit yourselves unto your own husbands, as it is fit

in (the) Lord.
19 Husbands, love the
wives and do not be bit-
ter against them.
20 Children, obey the
parents in all things, for
this is pleasing to the
Lord.
21 Fathers, do not pro-
voke your children, that
they may not be dis-
heartened.
22 Slaves, obey the
lords according to flesh
in all things, not with
eye-service as men-
pleasers, but in single-
ness of heart, fearing
God.

23 And (in) everything,
whatever you may do,
work from the soul as to
the Lord and not to men.
24 knowing that from
the Lord you shall re-
ceive the reward of the
inheritance. For you
serve the Lord Christ.

25 But the (one) doing
wrong will receive
what he did wrong, and
there (is) not respect of
faces.

433   1722 2962   3588 435   25   3588   1135   2532 3361
ἀνῆκεν ἐν Κυρίῳ. 19 οἱ ἄνδρες, ἀγαπᾶτε τὰς γυναῖκας, καὶ μὴ
becoming in (the) Lord. The husbands, love   the   wives,   and not
4087   4314 846   3588 5043   5219   3588   1118
πικραίνεσθε πρὸς αὐτάς. 20 τὰ τέκνα, ὑπακούετε τοῖς γονεῦσι
be bitter   against them.   The children, obey   the   parents
2596 3956   5124 1063 2076   2101   3588 2962   3588
κατὰ πάντα· τοῦτο γάρ ἐστιν εὐάρεστον τῷ Κυρίῳ. 21 οἱ
according to all: this for is   well-pleasing to the Lord.   The
2962   3361 2042   3588 5043   5216 2443 3361   120   3588
πατέρες, μὴ ἐρεθίζετε τὰ τέκνα ὑμῶν, ἵνα μὴ ἀθυμῶσιν. 22 οἱ
fathers, not do provoke the children of you, that not they be dispirited. The
1401   5219   2596 3956 3588 2596   4561 2962   3361/1722
δοῦλοι, ὑπακούετε κατὰ πάντα τοῖς κατὰ σάρκα κυρίοις, μὴ ἐν
slaves.   obey   according to all things those according to flesh lords, not with
3787   5613   441   235 1722   572   2588
ὀφθαλμοδουλείαις ὡς ἀνθρωπάρεσκοι, ἀλλ᾽ ἐν ἁπλότητι καρ-
eye-service as   men-pleasers,   but in singleness of heart,

5399   3588 2316   2532 3956 3739 5100 1437   4160 1537
δίας, φοβούμενοι τὸν Θεόν· 23 καὶ πᾶν ὃ τι ἐὰν ποιῆτε, ἐκ
fearing   God   And (in)everything whatever you do, from
5590   2038   5613 3588 2962 2532 3756   444   1492
ψυχῆς ἐργάζεσθε, ὡς τῷ Κυρίῳ καὶ οὐκ ἀνθρώποις· 24 εἰδότες
(the) soul work,   as to the Lord and not to men.   knowing
3754 575   2962   618   3588   469   3588   2817
ὅτι ἀπὸ Κυρίου ἀπολήψεσθε τὴν ἀνταπόδοσιν τῆς κληρονο-
that from (the) Lord you will receive the   reward   of the inheritance.
3588 1063 2962   5547   1398   3588 1063   91
μίας· τῷ γὰρ Κυρίῳ Χριστῷ δουλεύετε. 25 ὁ δὲ ἀδικῶν
the For Lord Christ   you serve.   he And doing wrong
2865 3739 91   2532 3756 2076   4382
κομιεῖται ὃ ἠδίκησε· καὶ οὐκ ἔστι προσωποληψία.
will receive what he did wrong, and not (is) respect of faces.

in the Lord.
19 Husbands, love
(your) wives, and be not
bitter against them.
20 Children, obey
(your) parents in all
things: for this is well
pleasing unto the Lord.
21 Fathers, provoke not
your children (to an-
ger), lest they be dis-
couraged.
22 Servants, obey in all
things (your) masters
according to the flesh;
not with eyeservice, as
menpleasers; but in sin-
gleness of heart, fearing
God:

23 And whatsoever ye
do, do (it) heartily, as to
the Lord, and not unto
men;
24 Knowing that of the
Lord ye shall receive
the reward of the inheri-
tance: for ye serve the
Lord Christ.

25 But he that doeth
wrong shall receive for
the wrong which he
hath done: and there is
no respect of persons.

Acrostic Index

The following is the full chapter, in English and in Greek of First John: Chapter 3, Verse 17, where acrostic 11 begins, is clearly marked.

1. See what manner of love the Father has given us, that we may be called children of God. For this reason the world does not know us, because it did not know Him.

2 Beloved, now we are the children of God, and it was not yet revealed what we shall be. But we know that if He is revealed, we shall be like Him, because we shall see Him as He is.

3. And everyone having this hope on Him purifies himself even as that (One) is pure.

4 Everyone practicing sin also practices lawlessness, and sin is lawlessness.

5 And you know that (One) was revealed that He might take away our sins, and sin is not in Him.

6 Everyone abiding in Him does not sin. Everyone sinning has not seen Him, nor known Him.

7 Little children, let no one lead you astray; the (one) practicing righteousness is righteous, even as that One is righteous.

8 The (one) practicing sin is of the devil, because the devil sins from (the) beginning. For this the Son of God was revealed, that He undo the works of the devil.

9 Everyone who has been generated of God does not sin, because His seed abides in him, and he is not able to sin, because he has been generated of God.

1492	4217	26	1325	2254 3588 3962	2443	5043	

1. ἴδετε ποταπὴν ἀγάπην δέδωκεν ἡμῖν ὁ πατήρ, ἵνα τέκνα
See what manner of love has given us the Father, that children

2316   2564   1223 5124 3588 2889   3756   1097   2248   3754
Θεοῦ κληθῶμεν, διὰ τοῦτο ὁ κόσμος οὐ γινώσκει ἡμᾶς, ὅτι
of God we may be called. Therefore the world not knows us because

3756 1097   846   27   3568 5043 2316   2070 2532 3768
οὐκ ἔγνω αὐτόν. 2 ἀγαπητοί, νῦν τέκνα Θεοῦ ἐσμέν, καὶ οὔπω
not it knew Him. Beloved, now children of God we are, and not yet

5319   5100 2071   1492 1161 3754 1437   5319   3664
ἐφανερώθη τί ἐσόμεθα· οἴδαμεν δὲ ὅτι ἐὰν φανερωθῇ, ὅμοιοι
was it revealed what we shall be; we know but that if He is revealed, like

846   2071   3754 3700   846   2531   2076   2532 3956 3588
αὐτῷ ἐσόμεθα, ὅτι ὀψόμεθα αὐτὸν καθώς ἐστι. 3 καὶ πᾶς ὁ
Him we will be, because we will see Him as He is. And everyone

2192 3588   1680   3778   1909   846   48   1438   2531
ἔχων τὴν ἐλπίδα ταύτην ἐπ᾿ αὐτῷ ἁγνίζει ἑαυτόν, καθὼς
having hope this on Him purifies himself, even as

1565   53   2076   3956 3588 4160   3588   266   2532 3588
ἐκεῖνος ἁγνός ἐστι. 4 πᾶς ὁ ποιῶν τὴν ἁμαρτίαν, καὶ τὴν
that One pure is. Everyone practicing sin, also

458   4160 2532 3588 266   2076 3588 458   2532 1492   3754
ἀνομίαν ποιεῖ· καὶ ἡ ἁμαρτία ἐστὶν ἡ ἀνομία. 5 καὶ οἴδατε ὅτι
lawlessness practices, and sin is lawlessness. And you know that

1565   5319   2443 5100 266   2257 142 2532   264
ἐκεῖνος ἐφανερώθη, ἵνα τὰς ἁμαρτίας ἡμῶν ἄρῃ· καὶ ἁμαρτία
that (One) was revealed, that the sins of us He might take away, and sin

1722 846   3756 2076   3956/3588/1722/846   3306   3756   264   3956/3588
ἐν αὐτῷ οὐκ ἔστι. 6 πᾶς ὁ ἐν αὐτῷ μένων οὐχ ἁμαρτάνει· πᾶς ὁ
in Him not is. Everyone in Him abiding not sins; everyone

264   3756   3708   846   3761   1097   846
ἁμαρτάνων οὐχ ἑώρακεν αὐτόν, οὐδὲ ἔγνωκεν αὐτόν.
sinning not has seen Him, nor known Him.

5040   3367   4105   5209 3588 4160   3588   1343
7 τεκνία, μηδεὶς πλανάτω ὑμᾶς· ὁ ποιῶν τὴν δικαιοσύνην
Little children, no one let lead astray you; the (one) practicing righteousness

1342   2076   2531   1565   1342   2076   3588 4160 3588
δίκαιός ἐστι, καθὼς ἐκεῖνος δίκαιός ἐστιν· 8 ὁ ποιῶν τὴν
righteous is, even as that (One) righteous is; the (one) practicing

266   1537 3588   1228   2076 3754 575   746 3588   1228
ἁμαρτίαν ἐκ τοῦ διαβόλου ἐστίν, ὅτι ἀπ᾿ ἀρχῆς ὁ διάβολος·
sin of the devil is, because from beginning the devil

264   1519 5124   5319   3588 5207 3588   2316 2443 3089
ἁμαρτάνει. εἰς τοῦτο ἐφανερώθη ὁ υἱὸς τοῦ Θεοῦ, ἵνα λύσῃ
sins For this was revealed the Son of God, that He undo

3588 2041 3588   1228   3956 3588   1080   1537 3588 2316
τὰ ἔργα τοῦ διαβόλου. 9 πᾶς ὁ γεγεννημένος ἐκ τοῦ Θεοῦ
the works of the devil. Everyone having been generated of God

266   3756 4160   3754   4690   846 1722 846   3306   2532 3756
ἁμαρτίαν οὐ ποιεῖ, ὅτι σπέρμα αὐτοῦ ἐν αὐτῷ μένει· καὶ οὐ
sin not does, because seed of Him in him abides, and not

1410   264   3754 1537 3588 2316   1080   1722 5129
δύναται ἁμαρτάνειν, ὅτι ἐκ τοῦ Θεοῦ γεγέννηται. 10 ἐν τούτῳ

1. Behold, what manner of love the Father hath bestowed upon us, that we should be called the sons of God. Therefore the world knoweth us not, because it knew him not.

2 Beloved, now are we the sons of God, and it doth not yet appear what we shall be: but we know that, when he shall appear, we shall be like him; for we shall see him as he is.

3. And every man that hath this hope in him purifieth himself, even as he is pure.

4 Whosoever committeth sin transgresseth also the law: for sin is the transgression of the law.

5 And ye know that he was manifested to take away our sins; and in him is no sin.

6 Whosoever abideth in him sinneth not: whosoever sinneth hath not seen him, neither known him.

7 Little children, let no man deceive you: he that doeth righteousness is righteous, even as he is righteous.

8 He that committeth sin is of the devil; for the devil sinneth from the beginning. For this purpose the Son of God was manifested, that he might destroy the works of the devil.

9 Whosoever is born of God doth not commit sin; for his seed remaineth in him: and he cannot sin, because he is born of God.

10 In this

5318   2076 3588 5043   3588   2532 3588 5043   3588   1228
φανερά ἐστι τὰ τέκνα τοῦ Θεοῦ καὶ τὰ τέκνα τοῦ διαβόλου·
revealed are the children of God and the children of the devil;

the children of God and the children of the devil are revealed. Everyone not practicing righteousness is not of God; also the (one) not loving his brother.
11. Because this is the message which you heard from (the) beginning, that we should love one another.

3956 3588 3361 4160   1343   3756 2076 1537 3588 2316 2532 3588 3361
πᾶς ὁ μὴ ποιῶν δικαιοσύνην οὐκ ἔστιν ἐκ τοῦ Θεοῦ, καὶ ὁ μὴ
everyone not practicing righteousness not is   of   God, also he not

25   3588 80   846   3754 3778 2076 3588 31   3759
ἀγαπῶν τὸν ἀδελφὸν αὐτοῦ. 11 ὅτι αὕτη ἐστὶν ἡ ἀγγελία ἣν
loving the brother of him Because this is   the message which

191   575   746   2443   25   240   3756 2531
ἠκούσατε ἀπ᾽ ἀρχῆς, ἵνα ἀγαπῶμεν ἀλλήλους· 12 οὐ καθὼς
you heard from beginning, that we should love one another;   not as

12 not as Cain was of the evil, and killed his brother. And for what did he kill him? Because his works were evil, but the things of his brother (were) righteous.

2535 1537 3588 4190   2258 2532 4969 3588   80   846   2532
Κάϊν ἐκ τοῦ πονηροῦ ἦν, καὶ ἔσφαξε τὸν ἀδελφὸν αὐτοῦ. καὶ
Cain of the evil   was, and killed the brother of him And

5484   5101 4969   846   3754 3588 2041   846   4190   2258
χάριν τίνος ἔσφαξεν αὐτόν; ὅτι τὰ ἔργα αὐτοῦ πονηρὰ ἦν,
for   what did he kill him? Because the works of him evil   were,

3588 1161 3588   80   846 1342
τὰ δὲ τοῦ ἀδελφοῦ αὐτοῦ δίκαια.
the things but of the brother of him (were) righteous.

3361   2296   80   3450 1487 3404   5209 3588 2889
13 Μὴ θαυμάζετε, ἀδελφοί μου, εἰ μισεῖ ὑμᾶς ὁ κόσμος·
Not do marvel, brothers of me, if hates you the world.

13 Do not marvel, my brothers, if the world hates you.
14 We know that we have passed from death to life because we love the brothers. The (one) not loving the brother remains in death.

2249 1492   3754   3327   1537 3588 2288   1519 3588
14 ἡμεῖς οἴδαμεν ὅτι μεταβεβήκαμεν ἐκ τοῦ θανάτου εἰς τὴν
We   know   that we have passed from death   into

2222 3754   25   3588   80   3588 3361   25   3588   80
ζωήν, ὅτι ἀγαπῶμεν τοὺς ἀδελφούς. ὁ μὴ ἀγαπῶν τὸν ἀδελφόν,
life, because we love the brothers The (one) not loving the brother.

3306 1722 3588 2288   3956 3588 3404 3588   80   846   80
μένει ἐν τῷ θανάτῳ. 15 πᾶς ὁ μισῶν τὸν ἀδελφὸν αὐτοῦ ἀνθρω-
remains in death. Everyone hating the brother of him a murderer

15 Everyone hating the brother is a murderer, and you know that every murderer does not have everlasting life abiding in him.

2076 2532 1492   3754 3956   443   3756 2192
ποκτόνος ἐστί· καὶ οἴδατε ὅτι πᾶς ἀνθρωποκτόνος οὐκ ἔχει
is.   and you know that every murderer   not has

2222 166   1722 846   3306   1722 5129   1097   3588
ζωὴν αἰώνιον ἐν αὐτῷ μένουσαν. 16 ἐν τούτῳ ἐγνώκαμεν τὴν
life everlasting in him abiding. By this we have known the

16. By this we have known the love of God, because that (One) laid down His life on behalf of us; and on behalf of the brothers we ought to lay down (our) lives.

26   3588 2316 3754 1565   5228 2257 3588 5590   846
ἀγάπην τοῦ Θεοῦ, ὅτι ἐκεῖνος ὑπὲρ ἡμῶν τὴν ψυχὴν αὐτοῦ
love   of God, because that (One) on behalf of us the life   of Him

5087   2532 2249   3784   5228 3588   3784   3588 5590
ἔθηκε· καὶ ἡμεῖς ὀφείλομεν ὑπὲρ τῶν ἀδελφῶν τὰς ψυχάς
laid down: and we   ought   on behalf of the brothers the lives

5087   1739 1161 302 2192 3588 979 3588 2889   2532 2334 3588
τιθέναι. 17 ὃς δ᾽ ἂν ἔχῃ τὸν βίον τοῦ κόσμου, καὶ θεωρῇ τὸν
lay down   Whoever has the means of life of the world, and beholds the

17 Whoever has the means of life of the world, and sees his brother having need, and shuts up his bowels from him, how does the love of God abide in him?

80   846   5532 2192   2808   3588   4698
ἀδελφὸν αὐτοῦ χρείαν ἔχοντα, καὶ κλείσῃ τὰ σπλάγχνα
brother of him need   having, and shuts up the bowels

846   575   846   4459   575 26   3588 2316 3306 1722 846
αὐτοῦ ἀπ᾽ αὐτοῦ, πῶς ἡ ἀγάπη τοῦ Θεοῦ μένει ἐν αὐτῷ;
of him from him, how the love   of God abides in him?

18 My little children, let us not love in word, or in tongue, but in deed and in truth.

5040   3450 3361   25   3056 3366   1100   235   2041
18 τεκνία μου, μὴ ἀγαπῶμεν λόγῳ μηδὲ γλώσσῃ, ἀλλ᾽ ἔργῳ
Little children of me, not let us love in word nor in tongue, but in deed

2532 225   2532 1722 5129   1097   3754 1537 3588   225
καὶ ἀληθείᾳ. 19 καὶ ἐν τούτῳ γινώσκομεν ὅτι ἐκ τῆς ἀληθείας
and in truth.   And in this we shall know that of the truth

19 And in this we shall know that we are of the truth, and shall persuade our hearts before Him.

2070   2532   1715   846   3982   3588 2588   2257
ἐσμέν, καὶ ἔμπροσθεν αὐτοῦ πείσομεν τὰς καρδίας ἡμῶν,
we are, and before   Him shall persuade the heart   of us,

the children of God are manifest, and the children of the devil: whosoever doeth not righteousness is not of God, neither he that loveth not his brother.
11. For this is the message that ye heard from the beginning, that we should love one another.
12 Not as Cain, (who) was of that wicked one, and slew his brother. And wherefore slew he him? Because his own works were evil, and his brother's righteous

13 Marvel not, my brethren, if the world hate you.
14 We know that we have passed from death unto life, because we love the brethren. He that loveth not (his) brother abideth in death.
15 Whosoever hateth his brother is a murderer: and ye know that no murderer hath eternal life abiding in him.

16. Hereby perceive we the love (of God), because he laid down his life for us: and we ought to lay down (our) lives for the brethren.
17 But whoso hath this world's good, and seeth his brother have need, and shutteth up his bowels (of compassion) from him, how dwelleth the love of God in him?

18 My little children, let us not love in word, neither in tongue; but in deed and in truth.
19 And hereby we know that we are of the truth, and shall assure our hearts before him.

Literal Translation

20 that if our heart ac-
cuses us, (we know)
that God is greater than
our heart and knows all
things.
21 Beloved, if our heart
does not accuse us, we
have confidence with
God

22. And whatever we
ask, we receive from
Him, because we keep
His commandments,
and we do the things
pleasing before Him

23 And this is His com-
mandment, that we
should believe (on) the
name of His Son, Jesus
Christ, and love one an-
other, even as He gave
command to us.

24 And the (one) keep-
ing His command-
ments abides in Him,
and He in him. And by
this we know that He
abides in us, by the
Spirit which He gave to
us.

Greek interlinear

3754 1437 2607 2257 3588 2588 3754 3187 2076 3588
20 ὅτι ἐὰν καταγινώσκῃ ἡμῶν ἡ καρδία, ὅτι μείζων ἐστὶν ὁ
that if accuses of us the heart, that greater is

2316 3588 2588 2257 2532 1097 3956 27
Θεὸς τῆς καρδίας ἡμῶν, καὶ γινώσκει πάντα. 21 ἀγαπητοί,
God (than) the heart of us. and knows all things. Beloved,

1437 3588 2588 2257 3361 2607 2257 3954
ἐὰν ἡ καρδία ἡμῶν μὴ καταγινώσκῃ ἡμῶν, παρρησίαν
if the heart of us not accuses us, confidence

2192 4314 3588 2316 2532 3739 1437 154 2983 3844
ἔχομεν πρὸς τὸν Θεόν, 22 καὶ ὃ ἐὰν αἰτῶμεν, λαμβάνομεν παρ'
we have with God and whatever we ask, we receive from

846 3754 3588 1785 846 5083 2532 3588 701
αὐτοῦ, ὅτι τὰς ἐντολὰς αὐτοῦ τηροῦμεν, καὶ τὰ ἀρεστὰ
Him, because the commandments of Him we keep, and the things pleasing

1799 846 4160 2532 3778 2076 3588 1799 846
ἐνώπιον αὐτοῦ ποιοῦμεν. 23 καὶ αὕτη ἐστὶν ἡ ἐντολὴ αὐτοῦ,
before Him we do. And this is the commandment of Him,

2443 4100 3588 3686 3588 5207 846 2424 5547
ἵνα πιστεύσωμεν τῷ ὀνόματι τοῦ υἱοῦ αὐτοῦ Ἰησοῦ Χρι-
that we should believe (on) the name of the Son of Him Jesus Christ,

2532 25 240 2531 1325 1785 2254
στοῦ, καὶ ἀγαπῶμεν ἀλλήλους, καθὼς ἔδωκεν ἐντολὴν ἡμῖν.
and love one another, even as He gave command to us.

2532 3588 5083 3588 1785 846 1722 846 3306 2532 846 1722
24 καὶ ὁ τηρῶν τὰς ἐντολὰς αὐτοῦ ἐν αὐτῷ μένει, καὶ αὐτὸς ἐν
and (the) one keeping the commandments of Him in Him abides, and He in

846 2532 1722 5129 1097 3754 3306 1722 2254 1537 3588
αὐτῷ. καὶ ἐν τούτῳ γινώσκομεν ὅτι μένει ἐν ἡμῖν, ἐκ τοῦ
him. And by this we know that He abides in us, by the

4151 3739 2254 1325
Πνεύματος οὗ ἡμῖν ἔδωκεν.
Spirit which to us He gave.

King James Version

20 For if our heart con-
demn us, God is greater
than our heart, and
knoweth all things.
21 Beloved, if our heart
condemn us not, (then)
have we confidence to-
ward God.

22. And whatsoever
we ask, we receive of
him, because we keep
his commandments,
and do those things that
are pleasing in his sight.

23 And this is his com-
mandment, That we
should believe on the
name of his Son Jesus
Christ, and love one an-
other, as he gave us
commandment.

24 And he that keepeth
his commandments
dwelleth in him, and he
in him. And hereby we
know that he abideth in
us, by the Spirit which
he hath given us.

Acrostic Index

The following is the full chapter, in English and in Greek of Jude: Chapter 1, Verse 4, where acrostic 12 begins, is clearly marked.

ΙΟΥΔΑ
JUDE

THE EPISTLE
OF JUDE

ΕΠΙΣΤΟΛΗ   ΚΑΘΟΛΙΚΗ
EPISTLE   GENERAL

THE EPISTLE
OF JUDE

Jude

Jude

Jude

2455	2424	5547	1401	80	1161	2385

1. Ἰούδας Ἰησοῦ Χριστοῦ δοῦλος, ἀδελφὸς δὲ Ἰακώβου,
Jude of Jesus Christ a slave, brother and of James,

1. Jude, a slave of Jesus Christ, and brother of James, to the (ones) called in God the Father, having been set apart, and having been kept to Jesus Christ;

1. Jude, the servant of Jesus Christ, and brother of James, to them that are sanctified by God the Father, and preserved in Jesus Christ, (and) called:

3588 1722 2316   3962   37   2532 2424 5547   5083
τοῖς ἐν Θεῷ πατρὶ ἡγιασμένοις, καὶ Ἰησοῦ Χριστῷ τετηρη-
to those in God (the) Father having been set apart, and to Jesus Christ having been

2822   1656 5213 2532   1515 2532 26   4129
μένοις, κλητοῖς· 2 ἔλεος ὑμῖν καὶ εἰρήνη καὶ ἀγάπη πληθυνθείη.
kept. called. mercy to you and peace and love, be multiplied.

2 mercy and peace and love be multiplied to you

2 Mercy unto you, and peace, and love, be multiplied.

27   3956   4710   4160   1125   5213 4012
3. Ἀγαπητοί, πᾶσαν σπουδὴν ποιούμενος γράφειν ὑμῖν περὶ
Beloved, all diligence making to write to you about

3 Beloved, making all diligence to write to you about the common salvation, I had need to write to you exhorting (you) to contend earnestly for the faith once delivered to the saints.

3 Beloved, when I gave all diligence to write unto you of the common salvation, it was needful for me to write unto you, and exhort (you) that ye should earnestly contend for the faith which was once delivered unto the saints.

3588 2839   4991   318   2192   1125   5213 3870
τῆς κοινῆς σωτηρίας, ἀνάγκην ἔσχον γράψαι ὑμῖν, παρα-
the common salvation, need I had to write to you, ex-

1864   3588 530   3860   3588   40
καλῶν ἐπαγωνίζεσθαι τῇ ἅπαξ παραδοθείσῃ τοῖς ἁγίοις.
horting to earnestly contend for the once delivered to the saints.

4102   3921   1063 5100   444   3588 3819   4270
πίστει 4 παρεισέδυσαν γάρ τινες ἄνθρωποι, οἱ πάλαι προγε-
faith. stole in For certain men, those of old having

4 For certain men stole in, those of old having been written before to this judgment, ungodly ones perverting the grace of God into unbridled lust, and denying the only Master, God, even our Lord Jesus Christ.

4 For there are certain men crept in unawares, who were before of old ordained to this condemnation, ungodly men, turning the grace of our God into lasciviousness, and denying the only Lord God, and our Lord Jesus Christ.

1519   5124 3588 2917   765   3588 3588 2316   2257
γραμμένοι εἰς τοῦτο τὸ κρίμα, ἀσεβεῖς, τὴν τοῦ Θεοῦ ἡμῶν
been written before to this judgment, ungodly (ones), the of the God of us

5485   3346   1519   766   2532 3588   3441   1203
χάριν μετατιθέντες εἰς ἀσέλγειαν, καὶ τὸν μόνον δεσπότην
grace perverting into unbridled lust, and the only Master

2316 2532   2962   2257   2424   5547   720
Θεόν, καὶ Κύριον ἡμῶν Ἰησοῦν Χριστὸν ἀρνούμενοι.
God, and Lord of us Jesus Christ denying.

5279   1161 5209   1014   1491   5209   530   5124
5. Ὑπομνῆσαι δὲ ὑμᾶς βούλομαι, εἰδότας ὑμᾶς ἅπαξ τοῦτο,
to remind And you I purpose, knowing you once this,

5. But I purpose to remind you, you once knowing these things, that the Lord having saved a people out of the land of Egypt, in the second place He destroyed the ones not believing.

5. I will therefore put you in remembrance, though ye once knew this, how that the Lord, having saved the people out of the land of Egypt, afterward destroyed them that believed not.

3754 3588 2962   2992 1537 1093   125   4982 3588   1208
ὅτι ὁ Κύριος, λαὸν ἐκ γῆς Αἰγύπτου σώσας, τὸ δεύτερον
that the Lord, a people out of land of Egypt having saved, in the second place

3588 3361   4100   622   32   5037 3588 3361
τοὺς μὴ πιστεύσαντας ἀπώλεσεν. 6 ἀγγέλους τε τοὺς μὴ
those not believing He destroyed. angels And those not

6 And those angels not having kept their first place, but having deserted their dwelling-place, He has kept in everlasting chains under darkness for the Judgment of a great day.

6 And the angels which kept not their first estate, but left their own habitation, he hath reserved in everlasting chains under darkness unto the judgment of the great day.

5083   3588   1438   746   235   620   3588
τηρήσαντας τὴν ἑαυτῶν ἀρχήν, ἀλλὰ ἀπολιπόντας τὸ
having kept the of themselves first place, but having deserted the

2398   3613   1519 2920   3173   2250   1199   126
ἴδιον οἰκητήριον, εἰς κρίσιν μεγάλης ἡμέρας δεσμοῖς ἀϊδίοις
own dwelling place, for (the) Judgment of a great day in chains eternal

5259 2217   5083   5613 4670 2532   1116   2532 3588 4012
ὑπὸ ζόφον τετήρηκεν. 7 ὡς Σόδομα καὶ Γόμορρα, καὶ αἱ περὶ
under blackness He has kept. As Sodom and Gomorrah, and those around

7 as Sodom and Gomorrah, and the cities around them, in like manner to these, committing fornication, and going away after other flesh, set before us an example, undergoing vengeance of everlasting fire.

7 Even as Sodom and Gomorrha, and the cities about them in like manner, giving themselves over to fornication, and going after strange flesh, are set forth for an example, suffering the vengeance of eternal fire.

846   4172   3588 3664   5125   5158   1608
αὐτὰς πόλεις, τὸν ὅμοιον τούτοις τρόπον ἐκπορνεύσασαι,
them cities, in the similar to these manner committing fornication,

2532   565   3694   4561   2087   4295   1164
καὶ ἀπελθοῦσαι ὀπίσω σαρκὸς ἑτέρας, πρόκεινται δεῖγμα,
and going away after flesh other, set before an example,

4442   166   1349   5254   3668   3305 2532   3778
πυρὸς αἰωνίου δίκην ὑπέχουσαι 8 ὁμοίως μέντοι καὶ οὗτοι
of fire everlasting vengeance undergoing. Likewise indeed also these

8. Likewise, indeed, also these

8. Likewise also these

www.ingramcontent.com/pod-product-compliance
Lightning Source LLC
Chambersburg PA
CBHW040131240726
48664CB00002B/440